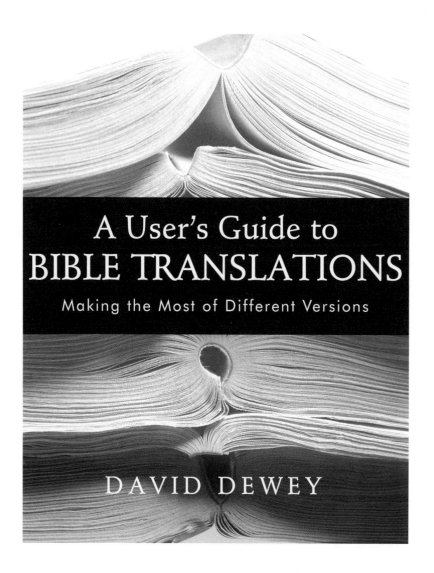

A User's Guide to
BIBLE TRANSLATIONS
Making the Most of Different Versions

DAVID DEWEY

InterVarsity Press
Downers Grove, Illinois

InterVarsity Press
P.O. Box 1400, Downers Grove, IL 60515-1426
Internet: www.ivpress.com
E-mail: mail@ivpress.com

InterVarsity Press® is the book-publishing division of InterVarsity Christian Fellowship/USA®, a student movement active on campus at hundreds of universities, colleges and schools of nursing in the United States of America, and a member movement of the International Fellowship of Evangelical Students. For information about local and regional activities, write Public Relations Dept., InterVarsity Christian Fellowship/USA, 6400 Schroeder Rd., P.O. Box 7895, Madison, WI 53707-7895, or visit the IVCF website at <www.intervarsity.org>.

The publisher has sought to ensure that the URLs for external websites referred to in this book are accurate and active at the time of going to press, but has no responsibility for such websites and cannot guarantee that any site will remain active or that its content is or will remain appropriate.

Copyright notices for Scripture versions used in this work can be found on pages 15-19.

The extract from The Alternative Service Book 1980 on page 204 is copyright © The Central Board of Finance of the Church of England 1980; The Archbishops' Council, 1999, and is reproduced by permission.

Cover design: Cindy Kiple

Cover image: Laurie Rubin/Getty Images

ISBN 0-8308-3273-4

Printed in the United States of America ∞

Library of Congress Cataloging-in-Publication Data
Dewey, David.
A user's guide to Bible translations: making the most of different
versions / David Dewey.
    p. cm
Includes bibliographical references and index.
ISBN 0-8308-3273-4 (alk. paper)
1. Bible. English—Versions—History. I. Title
BS455.D49 2004
220.5'2—dc22
                                                                2004025514

P	17	16	15	14	13	12	11	10	9	8	7	6	5	4	3	2	1
Y	17	16	15	14	13	12	11	10		09	08	07	06	05			

CONTENTS

INTRODUCTION

PART ONE: *The Task of Translation*

The Word of God in the Words of Men / The Art of Translation /
Accurate and Accessible; Reliable and Readable / Form-Driven and
Meaning-Driven Translations / Kernels of Meaning / A Spectrum of
Translations / Accuracy Again / Paraphrases

Vocabulary / Word Order and Complex Sentences / Connections /
Pronouns / Verb Forms and Tenses / Making Implicit Information
Explicit / Figures of Speech / Apparent Ambiguities / Miscellaneous
Features of Hebrew and Greek / Further Factors / Conclusions

Style in the Original / Reading Level / Formal Versus Conversational /
The Tyndale/King James Tradition / Bible English / Colloquialism
and Dialect / Verbosity / Reading Aloud / Memorability / Hebrew
Poetry / The Unity of Scripture / Visual Style

Bible (1962-1971) / Knox's Bible (1945-1955) / The Jerusalem Bible
(1966) / The New American Bible (1970)

The New American Standard Bible (1971) / Today's English Version
(1976) / The New International Version (1978) / The New King
James Version (1982) / The New Jerusalem Bible (1985) / The New
Century Version (1991); The International Children's Bible (1986) /
The Christian Community Bible (1988)

The Revised English Bible (1989) / The New Revised Standard
Version (1990) / The New Testament and Psalms: An Inclusive
Version (1995) / The New American Standard Bible Update (1995) /
God's Word (1995) / The New International Reader's Version (1994-
1998) / The Contemporary English Version (1995) / The New Living
Translation (1996; Revised 2004)

The Message (1993-2002) / The NIV Goes Inclusive (1997) / Today's
New International Version (2005) / The English Standard Version
(2001) / The Holman Christian Standard Bible (2004) / Bibles on the
Internet

The Wider Picture / The Personal Perspective

Transmission: The Old Testament / Transmission: The New
Testament / Textual Criticism / Disputed Passages

FOREWORD

When I was a young child in a Sunday-school class in the mid-1940s, the version of the Bible read to me was the Authorized Version of 1611. This classic version gave me a basic grounding in *the story* of the Bible, and I can still recall some of the verses I memorized as a boy.

When I was ordained as a minister in 1967, I was presented with a leather-bound copy of the 1952 Revised Standard Version of the Bible and given the charge to "preach the word . . . in season and out of season" (2 Timothy 4:2).

Thirty-five years after my ordination I have the New International Version of the New Testament on my handheld; I can download onto my computer Scripture passages from seventeen translations of the Bible.

As a child with my Authorized Version, I would never have understood the reason for a book called *A User's Guide to Bible Translations,* yet at the beginning of the twenty-first century there is an astonishing supermarket of Bible translations and paraphrases—which is why I warmly welcome this helpful primer to guide the reader in the search for a Bible version.

I have worked previously with David Dewey on writing projects that have required him to use his considerable skills of distilling complex technical information into plain language. He does not disappoint with this book. He distinguishes helpfully between form- and meaning-driven translations, and faces squarely the divisive controversy of inclusive language and gender accuracy. He provides an eminently readable overview of translations, from old English to Bibles on the Net, and concludes his book in the very best traditions of a survey, with some pointers to a shortlist of selected versions.

Once you have settled on your chosen version, the task has only just begun. You must read your translation of the Bible as if you were listening to a story for the very first time. Listen to God's story as if your life depended on it—*because it does.* The influence of the Bible through the centuries has been its power to evoke a passion for God's story.

In the early centuries, those who walked the pilgrim way from Iona to Lindisfarne would have learned the story from the panels on the Rothwell Cross with interpretive verses from the Latin Vulgate.

In the seventh century, the gifted Caedmon turned Scripture into poems which were celebrated in song, and another generation heard the story.

In the tenth century, King Alfred's last literary work was a translation of some of the Psalms. At the end of the same century, in the village of Eynsham in Oxfordshire, Aelfric was translating parts of the first seven books of the Bible.

The story lived on through the Middle Ages, despite the clergy's attempt to claim they had sole control of interpreting the mysteries of God's story. The courageous John Wycliffe not only asserted the authority of the Bible as being more important than clerical authority, he was convinced that every person should have access to a version of the Bible that they could understand. He and his followers were driven by this passion for God's story.

The prince of Bible translators, William Tyndale, shared the same passion and vowed to an educated opponent that "if God spares my life, I will cause a boy that drives a plough to know more of the scriptures than you do."

The Geneva Bible of 1560 was the translation that inspired John Bunyan in his passion to interpret the meaning of God's story in *Pilgrim's Progress.*

The awesome 1611 Authorized Version (AV) introduced millions of people to the story. In the years 1660-1710 alone, the 774,746 words of the AV (also known as the King James Version) went into 236 editions. This version in everyday language was an echo of the teaching of Jesus—"the common people heard him gladly" (Mark 12:37).

And so the story was carried into the twentieth century and then carried further by the explosion of translations and paraphrases that you can read about in *A User's Guide to Bible Translations.*

My prayerful hope for the twenty-first-century church is that we may learn a lesson from those who have gone before and ignite a renewed passion for God's story. This defining story has the power to refresh the church in its love for God and its mission in the world.

We desperately need a church that will spend less time on making the gospel relevant to the world and focus more on being a church that is relevant to the gospel.

The missionary church is at its best when it is a listening church.

David Coffey
General Secretary of the Baptist Union
Moderator of the Free Churches

ACKNOWLEDGMENTS

Gratitude is expressed to the editorial staff of IVP, both in Britain and the USA, for their hard work and careful editing. I'd also like to thank Margaret Berson, Clay Knick and Mark Strauss for their invaluable help: Margaret for commenting on early drafts of this book, Clay for tracking down reviews in American journals and Mark for his constructive criticisms. Gratitude also goes to members of Wayne Leman's online discussion forum for their interest and stimulating debates.

But this book is dedicated to Sarah: I could have no better partner in life or ministry.

PERMISSIONS

Amp.
Scripture quotations marked "Amp." are from the Amplified Bible. Copyright © 1965 by Zondervan Publishing House. All rights reserved.

CCB
Scripture quotations marked CCB are from the Christian Community Bible. Copyright © Bernardo Hurault 2000. Published by Pastoral Bible Foundation, Claretian Publications and St Pauls, Philippines.

CEV
Scripture quotations marked CEV are taken from the Contemporary English Version Bible, published by HarperCollins Publishers, © 1997 British and Foreign Bible. Used by permission.

ESV
Scripture quotations marked ESV are from The Holy Bible, English Standard Version, published by HarperCollins Publishers, © 2001 by Crossway Bibles, a division of Good News Publishers. Used by permission. All rights reserved.

GW
Scripture quotations marked GW are from the God's Word version. God's Word is a copyrighted work of God's Word to the Nations Bible Society. Copyright © 1995 by God's Word to the Nations Bible Society. All rights reserved.

HCSB
Scripture quotations marked HCSB are from the Holman Christian Standard Bible. © Copyright 1999, 2000, 2002, 2003 by Holman Bible Publishers. Used by permission.

ICB

Scripture quotations marked ICB are from the International Children's Bible, New Century Version, copyright © 1983, 1988 by Word Publishing. Anglicized Edition copyright © 1991 by Word (UK) Ltd, Milton Keynes, England. All rights reserved.

ISV

Scripture quotations marked ISV are from the International Standard Version. Copyright © 1996-2004 by the ISV Foundation. All rights reserved internationally.

JBP

Scripture quotations marked JBP are from J. B. Phillips's New Testament in Modern English. © J. B. Phillips 1947-1960, 1972. Published by Fount Paperbacks.

JB

Scripture quotations marked JB are from the Jerusalem Bible, © 1966 by Darton, Longman & Todd Ltd and Doubleday & Company, Inc.

LB

Scripture quotations marked LB are from the Living Bible. Copyright © 1971 Tyndale House Publishers. All rights reserved.

The Message

Scripture quotations marked *The Message* are copyright © 1993, 1994, 1995, 2000, 2001, 2002 by Eugene H. Peterson. Used by permission of NavPress Publishing Group. All rights reserved.

Moffatt

Scripture quotations marked "Moffat" are from James Moffatt, *A New Translation of the Bible*. Copyright © 1922, 1924, 1925, 1926, 1935, HarperCollins, San Francisco. Copyright © 1950, 1952, 1953, 1954, James A. R. Moffatt.

NAB

Scripture quotations marked NAB are taken from the New American

Bible Society. Used by permission of Hodder & Stoughton, a division of Hodder Headline Ltd. All rights reserved.

NIV

Scripture quotations marked NIV are taken from the Holy Bible, New International Version. Copyright © 1973, 1978, 1984 by International Bible Society. Used by permission of Zondervan Publishing House. All rights reserved.

NIVi

Scripture quotations marked NIVi are taken from the Holy Bible, New International Version. Copyright © 1973, 1978, 1984 by International Bible Society. First published in Great Britain in 1979. Inclusive language version 1995, 1996. Used by permission of Hodder & Stoughton, a division of Hodder Headline Ltd. All rights reserved. "NIV" is a trademark of International Bible Society. UK trademark number 1448790.

NKJV

Scripture quotations marked NKJV are from the New King James Version. Copyright © 1982 by Thomas Nelson, Inc. Used by permission.

NLT

Scripture quotations marked NLT are taken from the Holy Bible, New Living Translation, copyright © 1996, 2004. Anglicized version, copyright © 2000. Used by permission of Tyndale House Publishers, Inc., Wheaton, Illinois, 60189, USA. All rights reserved.

NRSV

Scripture quotations marked NRSV are taken from the New Revised Standard Version of the Bible, Anglicized edition, copyright © 1989, 1995 by the Division of Christian Education of the National Council of the Churches of Christ in the USA. Used by permission. All rights reserved.

RSV

Scripture quotations marked RSV are taken from the Revised Standard

Version, copyrighted 1946, 1952, © 1971, 1973, by the Division of Christian Education, National Council of the Churches of Christ in the USA, and used by permission.

REB
Scripture quotations marked REB are taken from the Revised English Bible, © Oxford University Press and Cambridge University Press 1989.

TEV
Scripture quotations marked TEV are taken from Today's English Version published by The Bible Societies/HarperCollins Publishers Ltd UK, © American Bible Society, 1966, 1971, 1976, 1992.

TNIV
Scripture quotations marked TNIV are taken from the Holy Bible, Today's New International Version. Copyright © 2001 by International Bible Society. All rights reserved.

LIST OF ABBREVIATIONS

A key to the abbreviations used for different Bible versions is found on page 26.

General Abbreviations

b.	born
c.	circa, about
chap(s).	chapter(s)
d.	died
DSS	Dead Sea Scrolls
ed(s).	editor(s), edited by, edition
et al.	and others
LXX	The Septuagint
MT	Masoretic Text
NT	New Testament
OT	Old Testament
p	papyrus
p(p).	page(s)
v(v).	verse(s)

Books of the Bible

Gen	Genesis
Ex	Exodus
Lev	Leviticus
Num	Numbers
Deut	Deuteronomy
Josh	Joshua
Judg	Judges
Ruth	
1, 2 Sam	1, 2 Samuel
1, 2 Kings	
1, 2 Chron	1, 2 Chronicles
Ezra	
Neh	Nehemiah
Esther	
Job	
Ps	Psalms
Prov	Proverbs

Eccles	Ecclesiastes
Song	Song of Songs
Is	Isaiah
Jer	Jeremiah
Lam	Lamentations
Ezek	Ezekiel
Dan	Daniel
Hos	Hosea
Joel	
Amos	
Obad	Obadiah
Jon	Jonah
Mic	Micah
Nahum	
Hab	Habakkuk
Zeph	Zephaniah
Hag	Haggai
Zech	Zechariah
Mal	Malachi
Mt	Matthew
Mk	Mark
Lk	Luke
Jn	John
Acts	
Rom	Romans
1, 2 Cor	1, 2 Corinthians
Gal	Galatians
Eph	Ephesians
Phil	Philippians
Col	Colossians
1, 2 Thess	1, 2 Thessalonians
1, 2 Tim	1, 2 Timothy
Tit	Titus
Philem	Philemon
Heb	Hebrews
Jas	James
1, 2 Pet	1, 2 Peter
1, 2, 3 Jn	1, 2, 3 John
Jude	
Rev	Revelation

INTRODUCTION

I do not make a habit of eavesdropping, but curiosity got the better of me on one occasion. I was quietly browsing the solitary shelf of Christian books in a local bookshop when a young woman appeared, looking for a Bible. She was clearly a new Christian; she had that wonderful new-born glow a pastor instantly recognizes. But her search seemed in vain. Several Bibles in different versions were available, but apparently not the one she wanted.

Approaching the counter, the woman explained she was looking for a Bible that was the same as the one used in her church. What translation was it? She didn't know, but it had a red cover, a dictionary-thingy at the back and some nice drawings. More important, she found it very easy to read. I guessed she meant a Today's English Version, complete with the delightful line-drawings of Swiss artist Annie Vallotton. But the assistant did not have a clue. He listened sympathetically for a while. Did she know the exact title? The publisher? Or . . . (wait for it!) . . . the author? After a while he sighed in resignation, "Well, madam, if it's not on the shelf, then we haven't got it." The young woman, still smiling in that disarming way brand-new Christians have, left to get better details from her minister.

Had the young woman gone to a specialty Christian bookshop, she would have got better advice. But she would have faced an even greater, near-overwhelming, choice: paperback, hardback or leather-bound—or even an electronic Bible on CD-ROM. With or without cross-references. With or without a concordance. With or without study notes, maps, the words of Christ in red, the Apocrypha. With or without any of a hundred and one other special features.

Buying a Bible can be intensely personal. Physically it is only a book, but a book that is the living Word of the living God. It is a decision we want to get right: a Bible can be a spiritual companion for many years, even a lifetime.

While we like to think the choices we make are logical, they rarely are. Buying a Bible is a matter of head *and* heart. I have known people who buy a Bible entirely on the basis of its color or cover design. For others, factors such as print size, durability and weight are of key importance. As for me, I must admit I love the wonderful feel and smell of a leather Bible. But there is a limit to how long you can stand in a bookshop sniffing every Bible in turn before attracting some strange stares!

This book's chief concern is with which translation to buy. Research undertaken by the Bible Society of England and Wales suggests Christians typically try out an unfamiliar translation for up to five years, using it alongside one they know and trust, before making the new translation their principal Bible.

Today, a typical Christian bookshop stocks between fifteen and twenty different English versions of the Bible. Go to the Internet and the list of available translations climbs to thirty or more. Not only is the choice confusing, it is almost immoral. Why should any language have two Bibles, let alone twenty or thirty, when so many languages—over four thousand—have none? Worldwide, 400 million people do not yet have even a single sentence of the Scriptures in their native tongue.

However we feel about having so many translations of God's Word in English, the fact is they are there, and more are promised. During the course of writing this book, four new English Bibles were launched, and several more new versions or revisions are due in the next two years.[1]

Given that English is now a truly global language, the glut of translations is perhaps not so surprising or altogether without justification. For some, the Bible *is* the 1611 King James Version, also known as the Authorized Version. But when it was translated, there were fewer than 6 million English speakers in the world, and perhaps fewer than one in four of these could actually read the Bible for themselves; the rest had to rely on listening to it read aloud, either in church or gathered around the table at home.

Today, there are around 600 million who use English as their first language and twice that number for whom it is their second language. Bibles are needed for liturgical and church use, for private and devotional reading, for academic study, for evangelism. Versions are required for highly literate readers and for children, for theologians and for those who have never opened a Bible before. Even if we do not need as many as we have, no single translation can meet all those diverse needs. But which Bible to choose?

THE RIGHT BIBLE

Listen in on any discussion about Bible translations and two questions always surface: Why so many? Which is best? This book will answer the first of these questions, and it *may* help to answer the second. The Bible that is best for you is not necessarily the one that is best for me. The one that is appropriate for reading aloud in church may not be suitable for private devotion or personal study. The one that suits a long-established Christian may not meet the needs of the inquirer or new believer.

This book has two main sections. Part one deals with the principles involved in Bible translation. Part two traces the story of how the Bible came to us. Less space is given to older and more obscure translations, while greater attention is paid to the most popular translations currently available; readers will undoubtedly want to know more about their favorite version![2]

In the concluding chapter, I look at current trends in English Bible translation and attempt to reach some conclusions as to which version might be best for you. (But don't turn to that final chapter just yet; you will spoil the plot!) There are also some appendixes containing technical information and reference material.

BIBLES AND THEIR ABBREVIATIONS

Bible translations are often referred to by their abbreviations. With so many versions around, you might think that the various combinations of letters are close to running out! Below is a list of the major translations you are likely to meet in the English-speaking world, together with the abbreviations used in this book. They appear below in date order. All are discussed in part two, and many are cited in part one to illustrate various points of translation theory.

AV/KJV	Authorized (King James) Version (1611)
RV	Revised Version (1885)
ASV	American Standard Version (1901)
RSV	Revised Standard Version (1952)
JBP	J. B. Phillips's New Testament in Modern English (1958; rev. 1972)
NWT	New World Translation (1961)
Amp.	Amplified Bible (1965)
JB	Jerusalem Bible (1966)
NEB	New English Bible (1970)
NAB	New American Bible (1970)
LB	Living Bible (1962-1971)
NASB	New American Standard Bible (1971)
TEV	Today's English Version (1976)
NIV	New International Version (1978)
NKJV	New King James Version (1982)
NJB	New Jerusalem Bible (1985)
ICB	International Children's Bible (1986)
CCB	Christian Community Bible (1988)
REB	Revised English Bible (1989)
NRSV	New Revised Standard Version (1990)
NCV	New Century Version (1991)
GW	God's Word (to the Nations) (1995)
CEV	Contemporary English Version (1995)
NASBu	New American Standard Bible update (1995)
NLT	New Living Translation (1996; rev. 2004)
NIrV	New International Readers Version (1994-1998)
NIVi	NIV inclusive-language edition (1997)
NET	New English Translation (2001)
NTPI	New Testament and Psalms: An Inclusive Version (1995)
ESV	English Standard Version (2001)
The Message	Eugene Petersen's The Message (1993-2002)
HCSB	Holman Christian Standard Bible (2004)
TNIV	Today's New International Version (2005)

Major English translations of the Bible. Dates reflect the complete Bible (i.e., New and Old Testaments).

PART ONE
The Task of Translation

1

THE TRANSLATOR'S ART

The Holy Scriptures . . . are able to make you wise for salvation through faith in Christ Jesus. All Scripture is God-breathed and is useful for teaching, rebuking, correcting and training in righteousness, so that all God's people may be thoroughly equipped for every good work.

2 TIMOTHY 3:15-17 TNIV

&

The Bible, Christians affirm, is God's inspired Word (2 Tim 3:16; cf. 2 Pet 1:20-21).[1] It is normative for Christian doctrine and practice. It shows us the way of salvation (2 Tim 3:15), and in its life-giving words we meet the living Word, Jesus Christ (Jn 5:39). But the Bible did not drop from the sky—and certainly not in English. The sixty-six separate books it contains all had to be written by someone—in fact, around forty "someones" over a time span of around one and a half millennia. The Bible has one divine author but many human authors, who wrote in the languages they knew: Greek for the New Testament and Hebrew (with a smattering of Aramaic)[2] for the Old Testament. And unless you are prepared to learn these ancient languages, you must use a translation to access the Word of God.

THE WORD OF GOD IN THE WORDS OF MEN

Though dubbed "the noblest monument of English prose,"[3] the Bible is anything but English, and it comes from a distant past and a remote culture. The challenges facing the translator cannot be overestimated.

We first turn our attention to the Bible's original languages.

Biblical Hebrew. Hebrew belongs to the Semitic group of languages, the most widely spoken of which today is Arabic. Like other Semitic tongues, Hebrew is written from right to left. It originally had no written vowels.

Hebrew, for a long time a dead language apart from its religious use within Jewish synagogues, has now been revived and is spoken in modern Israel. A Hebrew professor friend of mine once came back from Jerusalem with an official-looking piece of paper. He recognized a few Old Testament words: the document demanded he pay a certain number of shekels for his chariot. It turned out to be a parking fine!

Very little ancient Hebrew—only a few inscriptions—is found outside the Bible. A particular difficulty facing translators is the large number of words that occur only once or twice in the Old Testament, making it hard to be sure of their meaning. Translators often have to rely on similar words in other related ancient languages or depend on early translations of the Hebrew Bible into other languages such as the Greek Septuagint (see appendix one), the version of the Old Testament used by the early church and quoted in the New Testament.

Most Hebrew vocabulary is built up from root words of three consonants. Various prefixes and suffixes are added to these roots to indicate pronouns and prepositions. A Hebrew sentence, especially in poetry, may consist of only two or three words, but eight or nine English words may be necessary in translation. The particular forms of Hebrew poetry will be discussed on pages 83-85.

Hebrew has only two tenses: one for completed action, one for incomplete. But various verb forms can suggest different "moods," including the reflexive (e.g., to kill oneself) and the passive (to be killed). A verb can even be intensified in meaning; for example, *kill* can be strengthened to mean *massacre*. Many sentences have no verb at all; one has to be supplied for the sentence to make sense in English. Hebrew sentences are generally simple, often with a long series of narrative actions strung together with the word for *and*.

Many figures of speech appear in Hebrew. These make the language very expressive but also very down-to-earth; abstract concepts are largely avoided. The imagery of Hebrew is largely drawn from everyday life: a heroic person is a lion, a dependable person is a rock, and so on. Much of Hebrew imagery relates to parts of the body: the heart is the center of the will (not the emotions); one's kidneys ("reins" in the AV/KJV) the center of thought; and one's bowels(!) the center of affection.[4] It is obvious that great care must be taken in translating these expressions.

Some recognizable English words are in actuality Hebrew loan words, including *sabbath, jubilee, hallelujah* and *amen.*

New Testament Greek. Like Hebrew, Greek has its own alphabet, but it is a European language and is written from left to right. The Greek of the New Testament is not as elevated or polished as the more literary classical Greek dialects; it is known as *koinē* (or common) Greek. Until relatively recently, no written examples of *koinē* Greek were known outside the Bible, but archaeological discoveries have shown that it preceded Latin as the common language of business within the Roman Empire.

New Testament *koinē* Greek shows considerable Old Testament influence and contains a large number of Hebrew-style expressions and grammatical forms. The New Testament also contains a few untranslated Aramaic words: *abba*, meaning "father," is the best known.

Within the New Testament the quality of Greek varies. The most polished is found in Luke, Acts and Hebrews; the most torturous in 2 Peter and Jude. The Greek of Revelation is very stylized and full of Old Testament imagery. Paul's Greek (found in Romans-Philemon) is generally elegant, but he often writes in long, complex sentences. (Translating these can be like unraveling a tangled ball of string!)

Greek tenses do not entirely correspond to English expectations. Many verbs in the Gospel of Mark, for instance, are in the present tense. Translated as such, it would sound like a running commentary: "And now Jesus is healing the blind man, and now he is on his way to Jerusalem . . ." (a further example, Mk 1:40-45, is provided on pp. 53-

54).[5] Additionally, Greek uses far more participles—verbs ending in *ing*—than English, making it difficult to produce a natural rendering.

Well-known Greek words include *agapē* ("love"), *logos* ("word"), *apostolos* ("apostle") and *ekklēsia* ("church").

Before we pass on to translation methods, it needs to be pointed out that translators (as though they were not facing enough challenges already) cannot always be certain as to the original Hebrew or the original Greek, but must sift through the manuscript evidence in order to determine which "original" they are translating. This is called textual criticism and is discussed in appendix one.

THE ART OF TRANSLATION

Anyone who has ever tried to follow a set of assembly instructions poorly translated from Japanese or German will immediately appreciate that translation is not simply opening a bilingual dictionary and substituting every "foreign" word with a corresponding "English" one. If it were that easy, a computer could do in minutes what often takes a human being years to accomplish. Language is both more subtle and more complex than that. Moisés Silva stipulates:

> A successful translation requires: (1) mastery of the source languages—certainly a much more sophisticated knowledge than one can acquire over a period of four or five years; (2) superb interpretation skills and breadth of knowledge so as not to miss the nuances of the original; and (3) a very high aptitude for writing in the target language so as to express accurately both the cognitive and affective elements of the message.[6]

This list of priorities implies that a good command of Hebrew and Greek is more important than an ear sensitive to English expression. Recently, it has been suggested that these priorities should be reversed; that Bible translation might be done better by English experts, with the Hebrew and Greek scholars brought in simply to tidy up. That perhaps is going too far, but a good translation certainly must reflect high competency in English, not just Hebrew or Greek.[7]

ACCURATE AND ACCESSIBLE; RELIABLE AND READABLE

Those purchasing an untried Bible have two main concerns: is it reliable, and is it readable? Or put another way, is it both accurate and accessible? Translators differ as to how these concerns can best be met. Some argue for the merits of a literal translation; others favor a freer approach. *Literal* and *free* are, however, not the best terms to use; translators speak rather of "formal equivalence" and "functional (or 'dynamic') equivalence" respectively. There are several other terms in common use too, as shown in table 1.1.

Table 1.1. Alternative Descriptions of "Literal" and "Free" Categories

"Literal"	"Free"
formal equivalence	functional equivalence / dynamic equivalence
verbal equivalence	idiomatic translation
direct translation	indirect translation
word-for-word	thought-for-thought / sense-for-sense
form-based	meaning-based
form-driven	meaning-driven

All translations can be placed at some point on a line between extremely literal and extremely free. This is, in fact, the principal way of describing any particular Bible version. Where a translation is placed on this literal↔free spectrum determines into which of three categories it falls: word-for-word, thought-for-thought or paraphrase (see figure 1.1).

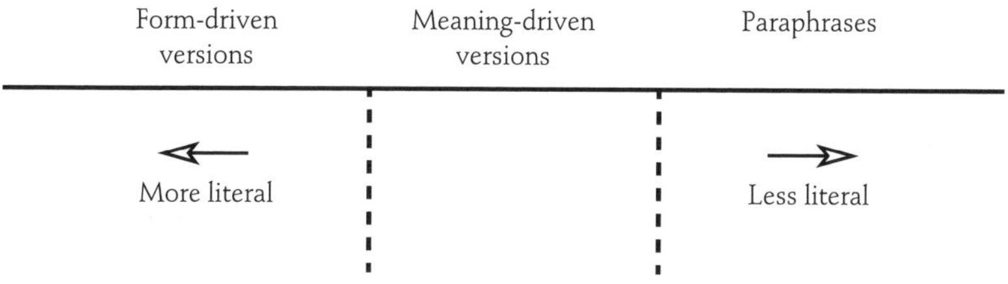

Figure 1.1. The literal-free spectrum

It is important to remember, however, that no translation is ever entirely one or the other. All show a degree of being form-driven and all a degree of being meaning-driven. Nevertheless, usually one or the other philosophy predominates. For the remainder of this book, I shall use the terms *form-driven* and *meaning-driven.*

Kevin Smith gives a good summary of the main differences between form- and meaning-driven translation approaches (see table 1.2).[8] His last two comparisons represent a value judgment. I will be exploring many of the points he raises over the next chapter and a half.

Table 1.2. Kevin Smith's Summary of Translation Approaches

Form-driven	Meaning-driven
Focuses on form	Focuses on meaning
Emphasizes source language	Emphasizes receptor language
Translates what was said	Translates what was meant
Presumes original context	Presumes contemporary context
Retains ambiguities	Removes ambiguities
Minimizes interpretive bias	Allows for interpretive bias
Awkward receptor-language style	Natural receptor-language style
Valuable for serious Bible study	Valuable for missionary use

FORM-DRIVEN AND MEANING-DRIVEN TRANSLATIONS

A form-driven translation is molded by the structure and style of the original language. Its aim is to come as close to the original as can be achieved in an English rendering. Where possible (depending on just how rigidly this translation philosophy is applied) a form-driven version will keep to the simple dictionary definitions of the Hebrew and Greek words being translated as well as the word order and grammatical structures of the original. If there is a long sentence in the Greek, a long sentence will appear in English, however awkward it may be.

In a meaning-driven version, however, the requirements of good, natural English determine the shape of the translation. A long Greek sentence may, for instance, be broken into several shorter English sentences. Word order may be rearranged, and a particular Greek or Hebrew word translated in different places by several different English words, depending on the context. A comparison will help. The New American Standard Bible (updated edition; NASBu) and the Contemporary English Version (CEV) were both published in 1995, but they could hardly be more different. The former is thoroughly form-driven, while the latter follows a rigorous meaning-driven approach. Both claim a high degree of accuracy. Table 1.3 shows a key theological passage in the two versions.

Table 1.3. Romans 3:21-26 in Two Versions

NASBu (italics in original)	CEV
[21]But now apart from the Law *the* righteousness of God has been manifested, being witnessed by the Law and the Prophets, [22]even *the* righteousness of God through faith in Jesus Christ for all those who believe; for there is no distinction; [23]for all have sinned and fall short of the glory of God, [24]being justified as a gift by His grace through the redemption which is in Christ Jesus; [25]whom God displayed publicly as a propitiation in His blood through faith. *This was* to demonstrate His righteousness, because in the forbearance of God He passed over the sins previously committed; [26]for the demonstration, *I say,* of His righteousness at the present time, so that He would be just and the justifier of the one who has faith in Jesus.	[21]Now we see how God makes us acceptable to him. The Law and the Prophets tell how we become acceptable, and it isn't by obeying the Law of Moses. [22]God treats everyone alike. He accepts people only because they have faith in Jesus Christ. [23]All of us have sinned and fallen short of God's glory. [24]But God treats us much better than we deserve, and because of Christ Jesus, he freely accepts us and sets us free from our sins. [25-26]God sent Christ to be our sacrifice. Christ offered his life's blood, so that by faith in him we should come to God. And God did this to show that in the past he was right to be patient and forgive sinners. This also shows that God is right when he accepts people who have faith in Jesus.

At even a cursory reading, certain differences in these two versions of Romans 3:21-26 are obvious. In contrast to the NASBu, the CEV employs more sentence breaks (ten as opposed to two) and easier vocabulary ("made acceptable to God" compared to "justified"; "set free from sins" rather than "redemption"; "sacrifice" as opposed to "propitiation") and is prepared to make significant changes to word order.

Often, a form-driven rendering is all that is needed to produce a perfectly sensible and natural translation. "In the beginning, God created the heavens and the earth" is a straightforward word-for-word rendering of Genesis 1:1 adopted by many translations. Why change it? Even Eugene Peterson's often voguish paraphrase *The Message* barely alters it: "First this: God created the Heavens and the Earth."

But elsewhere it is clear that a form-driven approach can lead to unintended, even humorous, results, such as the NIV's rendering of Psalm 1:1:

> Blessed is the man
> who does not walk in the counsel of the wicked
> or stand in the way of sinners
> or sit in the seat of mockers.

If you do not immediately see any difficulties with this verse, you probably have a high degree of familiarity with the Bible and have become immune to traditional Bible English or "biblish" (see pp. 79-80 for more on this). But put this verse in front of someone unacquainted with the Bible, and they will immediately spot several difficulties.

First, is God's blessing really just for men, or is it for women too? (I return to the question of inclusive language in chapter four.) Second, "standing in the way of sinners" is tantamount to obstructing their path, not copying their behavior, which is the intended meaning here. And finally, the complex threefold figure of speech "walk . . . stand . . . sit . . ." refers metaphorically to progressively deeper degrees in the imitation of sinful behavior. Table 1.4 demonstrates how two meaning-driven versions tackle Psalm 1:1.

Table 1.4. Psalm 1:1 in Two Meaning-Driven Translations

NLT (1996 and 2004)	CEV (1995)
Oh, the joys of those who do not follow the advice of the wicked, or stand around with sinners, or join in with mockers.	God blesses those people who refuse evil advice and won't follow sinners or join in sneering at God.

KERNELS OF MEANING

In comparison to form-driven versions, meaning-driven ones typically use easier vocabulary, shorter sentences and more natural English. All these points will be considered further in the next chapter, but none is actually central to the meaning-driven philosophy.

Key to a meaning-driven translation is the way a translator, rather than looking at single words or isolated expressions, takes as much as a whole paragraph, disassembles it, translates its constituent parts and then rebuilds it in the target language. Not all meaning-driven translations do this in the scientific kind of way described below. Many translators rely on their intuition to produce natural, idiomatic English, but a fully worked example will help.

Ephesians 1:7 in the RSV, NRSV and ESV runs thus: "In him [Christ] we have redemption through his blood, the forgiveness of our trespasses." The NIV is only a little different. In all these form-driven renderings, the word order and grammatical constructions are as they stand in the Greek; in English it is hard to grasp not only the meaning of each phrase but the relationship between them. If we break down what Paul is saying into its constituent parts (technically its "kernels of meaning"), we arrive at the following:

1. We trespassed (i.e., we wronged God, breaking his rules).
2. Christ shed his blood (i.e., he died sacrificially).
3. God redeems us (i.e., he frees us).
4. God forgives us.

Notice several things. First, we have put these kernels into their logical order. Second, the kernels have been expressed as a series of actions (e.g., "God redeems" instead of the more static "God gives redemption"). Third, the statements have been put into the active rather than the passive mood ("God forgives," not "We are forgiven"). If we now reassemble these elements in the simplest way possible, we arrive at the following: "We trespassed, but because of Christ's blood, God redeems us and forgives us."

For now the vocabulary is unchanged, but the order is much more logical. Here is how four meaning-driven translations tackle the same verse. Notice how they change the vocabulary as well as rearrange the various parts of the sentence:

NEB   By the death of Christ, we are set free and our sins forgiven.

TEV   By the death of Christ we are set free, that is, our sins are forgiven.

CEV   Christ sacrificed his life's blood to set us free, which means that our sins are now forgiven.

NLT   He [God] purchased our freedom with the blood of his Son and forgave our sins.

Compared to my attempt, all three have changed the construction of the verse less but the vocabulary more. Arguably, the CEV is the best of the four. If, going back to my attempt, we now simplify the vocabulary as well, we might arrive at something like this: "We wronged God, but because of Christ's sacrificial death, God frees us and forgives us."

In addition to the easier vocabulary, one piece of implicit information has been made explicit: Christ's "blood" becomes his "sacrificial death." Unless readers have some knowledge of the Old Testament, they will not realize that "through his blood" refers to death as a sacrifice. (See pp. 54-55 for more on making implicit information explicit.)

As will become apparent in part two in the review of English translations of the Bible in their historical order, most translations before 1900 fall into the form-driven category. Meaning-driven translations began appearing in the early twentieth century, but it is really only in the past forty years that a well-thought-out science of meaning-driven translation has been developed, largely as a result of the work of one man: Eugene Nida (b. 1914). Drawing on his experience of mission-field translation, he developed what he originally called "dynamic equivalence" translation but since 1986 has been termed "functional equivalence"—alternative expressions for what I am referring to as "meaning-driven translation."

Those translations that employ meaning-driven principles most consistently and that aim to make the Bible as accessible as possible, especially for inexperienced Bible readers, are sometimes called "common language" translations. Among these are Today's English Version (1976) and the Contemporary English Version (1995), both of which owe an enormous debt to Nida. In addition, the New Century Version (see p. 165) and God's Word translation (pp. 173-74) can be included under the category of "common language" translations.

Having said that meaning-driven translations are a relatively new phenomenon, William Tyndale, whose work underlies the King James Version of 1611, often adopted what, in retrospect, could be considered a meaning-driven approach. Even the AV/KJV is not as literal as many assume and is certainly not as literal as some more recent translations, for instance the NASB.

A SPECTRUM OF TRANSLATIONS

As we examine further the differences between form-driven and meaning-driven translations, certain points should be borne in mind.

First, *no translation is ever entirely literal or entirely free.* Perhaps the most literal translation ever published was Robert Young's in 1862, which translates John 3:16 as, "For God did so love the world, that His Son—the only begotten—He gave, that every one who is believing in him may not perish, but may have life age-during."

By keeping the English word order and tenses much as they are in the Greek, Young produced a rendering so literal that the result is almost unintelligible. It is certainly not English! And here is an important point: if a translation, however literal, cannot be understood, it cannot be said to be accurate. It has not done its job; it has not communicated the original meaning to today's audience.

Likewise, just as a translation that is form-driven in the extreme may not be accurate, so a translation that is very free may not be accurate. For example, in Clarence Jordan's *Cotton Patch New Testament* (1968), Paul's letter to the Romans is redirected "To Washington." While it is undoubtedly true that the good—and not so good—people of Washington, D.C., need the gospel every bit as much as those who once lived at the heart of earth's greatest empire, the *Cotton Patch* version cannot be deemed accurate. A translator cannot rewrite the historical setting of Scripture. Jordan's paraphrase is an exercise not merely in translation but in transculturation.

All translations employ a degree of freedom and a degree of literalness. Some clearly fall into the form-driven camp; others are without question meaning-driven; still others, like the NIV, sit somewhere in the middle. There is also the special category of "paraphrase" that I will consider at the end of the chapter.

A second point over which there is frequent misunderstanding is the common assumption that *there must be a trade-off between reliability (or accuracy) and readability (or accessibility)*. This is not necessarily true: a good translation will strive for both.

It is often thought that form-driven translations are reliable and meaning-driven versions readable. This leads to the suspicion that meaning-driven translations are less trustworthy and form-driven ones less readable. Chapter three will deal with readability, but first a little more on the subject of accuracy.

ACCURACY AGAIN

The accuracy of a translation is actually one of the more difficult criteria to measure. Other questions, such as ease of reading, choice of vocabulary and general style, can be assessed intelligently by sampling a few passages. But unless you know Hebrew and Greek, how can the degree of accuracy be ascertained?

Let me make two bold—and rather bald—statements, and then attempt to justify them:

1. No translation, however good, will ever be 100 percent accurate.
2. Most modern versions are highly accurate and very trustworthy.

These two statements may sound contradictory, but are not. First, no translation will ever be 100 percent accurate simply because no two languages ever express themselves in exactly the same way. It is not possible to carry every nuance of the original into clear English. Translation always involves a degree of compromise. Inevitably, something is lost, added or altered in the task of translating from one language to another. All translation involves at least a degree of interpretation. There is an old Italian proverb: *traduttore traditore* ("the translator is a traitor"). Unfortunately, it's true.

At this point some might feel uneasy. The Bible is indeed the inspired Word of God. The doctrine of inspiration, however, applies only to the *autographs*, or original manuscripts in the original languages, not to later copies or still later translations. Not one autograph still exists; thus, while God's providential hand is evident in the preservation, transmission and translation of the Bible, we have to allow for the fact that human error can creep in and has done so.

A pastor, so the story goes, introduced a modern version of the Bible into his church services. Afterward a parishioner complained, "If the King James Version was good enough for Saint Paul, then it's good enough for me!" But the AV/KJV was not the first Bible in English or the last, and it certainly has its fair share of translation mistakes.

Second, notwithstanding the above points, most modern translations *are* highly trustworthy. Of course, all translations *claim* to be accurate. While you might buy yogurt that claims to be 99 percent fat-free, no one is going to purchase a Bible that states on its cover that it is only 99 percent faithful to the original. But the fact is, so much effort—millions of dollars and thousands of hours—goes into a typical English translation that a high degree of accuracy is ensured. This is especially true of translations prepared by teams of translators constantly cross-checking each other's work. The accumulated scholarship is simply enormous. Apart from a few exceptions,[9] no modern English version contains any really dangerous inaccuracies, certainly none that impinge on our understanding of Christian doctrine. To be certain of the greatest possible accuracy, short of learning the original languages, the best approach is to compare one translation with another.

I did say most *modern* versions are highly accurate. There are three reasons why *older* translations, such as the AV/KJV, may not be:

1. Better Hebrew and Greek manuscripts have come to light.
2. Our understanding of Bible languages is constantly improving.

3. The English language is constantly changing.

But the question is how best to ensure that a modern translation is accurate and reliable. Here is a definition of accuracy:

> An accurate translation communicates to today's readers (or hearers) the same meaning that the original author's text conveyed to his original readers (or hearers).[10]

Once again we see that reliability cannot be separated from readability. A translation that is not readable is not reliable. If it cannot be understood, it cannot be said to be accurate. But while some argue that a form-driven approach is the best way to achieve the twin aims of reliability and readability, others stand by the philosophy of a meaning-driven approach.

This will be the subject of the next chapter, but to complete the present one, we need to consider a third category of translation: the paraphrase.

PARAPHRASES

Some Bibles are referred to as paraphrases. Best known are J. B. Phillips's New Testament in Modern English (1958, revised 1972; see pp. 150-51), Kenneth Taylor's Living Bible (completed in 1971; see pp. 151-52) and Eugene Peterson's *The Message* (completed in 2002; see pp. 182-83). Paraphrases are invariably the work of an individual rather than a team or committee.

Strictly speaking, a paraphrase is not a translation from one language to another but a rewording in the same language. While some paraphrases are in fact done this way (the Living Bible was paraphrased from the highly literal American Standard Version of 1901), others (such as the efforts of Phillips and Peterson) have been made directly from the original languages. I will use the term *paraphrase* to cover any free rendering, regardless or whether it was made from another English version or from the Greek and Hebrew.

It is not easy to make an entirely clear distinction between a paraphrase and other meaning-driven translations. But consider how three different translators might tackle one of the phrases from Psalm 23:5:

Form-driven	my cup overflows
Meaning-driven	my life overflows with blessing
Paraphrase	God blesses my socks off

Generally speaking, a paraphrase is marked by

- great freedom of vocabulary and expression
- a distinct language style, often very evocative, even quirky
- a willingness to use colloquialisms
- a tendency to be interpretive

Often a turn of a phrase wonderfully captures the meaning intended by the biblical author, but sometimes the accuracy of a paraphrase can leave much to be desired. For these reasons, while paraphrases can be helpful in giving a fresh and lively approach to Scripture, they can be recommended only as a secondary Bible, never a principal or sole translation. Additionally, paraphrases can and do date quickly.

The next chapter gives more detail about various aspects of translation and the different way form-driven and meaning-driven versions tackle them.

2

WORD-FOR-WORD OR
MEANING-FOR-MEANING?

Thy word is a lamp unto my feet, and a light unto my path.

PSALM 119:105 AV/KJV

✑

This chapter is a further look at the differences between form-driven and meaning-driven translations. Taking different aspects of the translation task in turn, we can see how these two philosophies vary in approach.

VOCABULARY

Compared to a form-driven approach, a meaning-driven philosophy looks at words in a different way. Meaning-driven translations use shorter, simpler words, and they translate words according to context, not just the standard dictionary definition.

Words, words, words. Consider the following: "The domesticated feline situated herself in a stationary and recumbent position on the diminutive floorboard covering." This is an unnecessarily long-winded way of saying, "The cat sat on the mat." Long, polysyllabic words are harder to understand than short words with just one or two syllables.

Most of English vocabulary comes from one of two sources: the Latin-based Romance languages (e.g., French and Spanish) and the northern Germanic languages (e.g., Anglo-Saxon and Danish). Words of Germanic origin tend to be shorter, and those of Romance origin longer; for example, *place* versus *situation, man* versus *person* and *friend* versus *companion*. In fact, the words that often make the strongest impact—swear words—are mostly Anglo-Saxon in origin. (They need not be quoted!)

Part of the genius of William Tyndale, whose work underlies the AV/KJV, was his ability to make an impact with simple words. More often than not, he chose short words and pithy phrases of a Germanic rather than Romance origin. The following, though preserved in the AV/KJV, are originally by Tyndale and have passed into the English language:

- "Let there be light" (Gen 1:3)
- "Am I my brother's keeper?" (Gen 4:9)
- "Ask and it shall be given you" (Mt 7:7)
- "The signs of the times" (Mt 16:3)
- "Where two or three are gathered" (Mt 18:20)
- "With God all things are possible" (Mt 19:26)
- "The spirit indeed is willing, but the flesh is weak" (Mt 26:41)
- "Eat, drink, and be merry" (Lk 12:19)
- "In him we live and move and have our being" (Acts 17:28)
- "The powers that be" (Rom 13:1)
- "Suffer fools gladly" (2 Cor 11:19)
- "Fight the good fight of faith" (1 Tim 6:12)
- "The patience of Job" (Jas 5:11)
- "Behold, I stand at the door and knock" (Rev 3:20)

As well as keeping the general vocabulary short and sharp to promote reading ease, there are also specific words that readers are unlikely to meet outside the context of the Bible. Take, for example, John the Baptist who came "preaching a baptism of repentance for the forgiveness of sin" (Mk 1:4). Here several words are strung together, some or even all of which may not make sense to a new Bible reader, *repentance* being the hardest. And we can think of plenty of other doctrinal words that are even harder: *justification, redemption, salvation* and *atonement,* to list only a few. *Expiation* and *propitiation* probably have no meaning at all to most people, yet the difference in nuance between them led to at least one translation being rejected by a large swath of Christians.[1]

Even short words like *sin* or *grace,* though recognized, may not be understood properly. To many, *sin* conjures up only the idea of sexual misbehavior or serious wrongdoing such as murder, whereas the Bible defines it as any behavior that falls short of the perfection demanded by God's glory, and counts it as a ruling principle in human life (see Rom 1—5). Likewise, *grace,* rather than suggesting the idea of God's undeserved kindness, may conjure up the idea of elegance, as in, "The ballerina danced with grace."

Three meaning-driven versions each tackle the word *repentance* in Mark 1:4 in a different way:

TEV   "John . . . preaching, Turn away from your sins and be baptized . . . and God will forgive your sins."

CEV   "John . . . told everyone, Turn back to God and be baptized! Then your sins will be forgiven."

NLT   John . . . preached that people should be baptized to show that they had turned to God to receive forgiveness for their sins.

Repentance is not a word in everyday use. It carries the specific theological meaning of (1) turning away from sin *and* (2) turning toward God. The TEV highlights only the former; the CEV only the latter. The NLT captures both, but at the cost of producing a long and wordy sentence.

With all vocabulary choices, translators must be clear about their target readership. Clearly, those with little or no prior knowledge of Bible truth are not likely to understand words like *justification, atonement* or *redemption,* as they are not employed much in everyday speech. But for the diligent Bible student there are advantages in using traditional Bible terminology. A single word like *justification* can, if properly understood, communicate a wealth of doctrinal truth very succinctly. Any substitution will almost invariably require an entire phrase: *justification* becomes "being made right with God"; *redemption* turns into "being set free from enslavement to sin."

In addition, these kinds of substitutions often divorce a theological concept from its original setting. Justification comes from the law courts; redemption from the slave market. When substitutions are used, these connections become less obvious or even entirely obscured. Along with such doctrinal words, a whole range of religious, historical and cultural words are found in Scripture, such as *apostle, ark of the covenant, circumcision, concubine, firstfruits, Gehenna, holy of holies, horn of salvation, leviathan, manna, remnant, Sanhedrin, tetrarch, tithe* and many, many more.

Proponents of form-driven translations argue that it *is not* the translator's task to provide any sort of interpretation or explanation of doctrinal, cultural or historical expressions; this task should be left to preachers and commentators. But is this the right approach? An Ethiopian official (introduced in Acts 8) was fortunate to have Philip climb aboard his chariot and help him understand the prophet Isaiah, but what about the person who picks up a Gideon Bible in a hotel bedroom or prison cell with no one there to explain its meaning? Or a person living in a country otherwise closed to the gospel who has tuned in to a Bible broadcast? Advocates of a meaning-driven approach argue it *is* appropriate for translators to make the Scriptures as understandable as possible to their intended readership.

The important phrase here is, of course, "intended readership." If the target reader or listener can understand words like *repentance, redemption* and *justification,* then such words provide a concise way of expressing deep and precious truths, but if not, alternative words or expressions need to be found.

Perhaps no translation (as opposed to paraphrase) has gone further than the CEV in exchanging traditional Bible vocabulary for words and phrases found in everyday life. Some examples from Romans 3 were noted on page 35; some other substitutions the CEV has made are listed in table 2.1. In addition, the CEV uses footnotes and a glossary to explain the meaning of other difficult words including historical and cultural references.

Table 2.1. Meaning-Driven Vocabulary in the CEV

Traditional Versions	CEV
make atonement	sacrifice one's life blood
sanctify	make holy
God's grace	God's (undeserved) kindness
gospel	good news
covenant	agreement
synagogue	Jewish meeting place
bishop/elder	church official/leader
parable	story

Generally speaking, form-driven translations retain traditional Bible vocabulary, while meaning-driven versions seek alternatives in order to make the Bible more accessible to readers who are less familiar with the Scriptures or who have a lower reading ability.

Dictionary definitions. Form-driven versions generally translate words according to their most obvious dictionary definition. In some extreme cases, they use exactly the same English word or phrase for every occurrence of a particular word or phrase in the original language. Technically, this is called *concordance*.[2] In contrast, meaning-driven versions generally translate each word or phrase in the original according to its context and not necessarily by the same English expression every time.

In English, one word may have two or more very different meanings in different contexts. I once asked a foster child staying in our home to draw the curtains. Her reply was that she had put away her crayons for the day and did not want to draw another picture. The word *draw* has at least two distinct meanings, but Dawn knew only one, while I was intending another. The phrase "drawing a gun" suggests a third; "to draw a line under something" a fourth, with both literal and metaphorical meanings. The variety of meanings a word can have is called its semantic range.

The Greek word *sarx* is especially bothersome to translators. It is one of the apostle Paul's most used words, and its simple dictionary definition is *flesh*. But in New Testament usage it has a wide semantic range. Mark Strauss cites verses giving evidence for at least ten different shades of meaning;[3] I shall note just three. Table 2.2 compares how the NRSV and NIV translate these verses.

Table 2.2. The Semantic Range of *Sarx*

Passage	NRSV	NIV	Meaning of *sarx*
Phil 1:22	If I am to live in the *flesh*, that means fruitful labor for me . . .	If I am to go on living in the *body*, this will mean fruitful labor for me . . .	the human body (morally neutral)
1 Cor 15:50	*flesh* and blood cannot inherit the kingdom of God . . .	*flesh* and blood cannot inherit the kingdom of God . . .	our mortal nature in contrast to God's eternal nature (morally neutral but weak and limited)
Gal 5:17	what the *flesh* desires is opposed to the Spirit . . .	the *sinful nature* desires what is contrary to the Spirit . . .	unrenewed human nature (morally corrupt and with a bias to sin)

Again, while it might seem obvious that it is better to translate according to context (and often it is), the advantages in keeping to one dictionary definition become especially evident when undertaking word studies or comparing one portion of text with another. The student with a form-driven translation knows that the same Greek word, *sarx,* appears in Philippians 1:22, 1 Corinthians 15:50 and Galatians 5:17; the person with a meaning-driven version cannot know this. For similar reasons, it is easier with a form-driven translation to see when a New Testament author is alluding to the Old Testament or when an epistle writer is picking up a thread from earlier in his letter. For an analysis of how often in translating Paul's letters the Greek word *sarx* is rendered as "flesh" in English, see table 2.3.

Table 2.3. Translation of *Sarx* **as "Flesh"**

Version	*Sarx* translated "flesh"*
NASBu	89 times
ESV	78 times
RSV	69 times
NRSV	65 times
TNIV	16 times
NIV	13 times
NLT	13 times

*The word *sarx* appears ninety-one times in Paul's letters.

The range of translation of *sarx* as reflected in table 2.3 corresponds closely with where these translations sit on the form-driven versus meaning-driven spectrum (see table 2.6 on p. 66). The most literal is the NASBu, and the least are the NIV and the NLT.

WORD ORDER AND COMPLEX SENTENCES

Word order plays a role in every language, but especially so in English. The newspaper headline "Dog Bites Man" suggests an everyday story; "Man Bites Dog" promises a truly rare event! While other languages use various grammatical indicators to distinguish between subject and object, English relies almost entirely on word order, the usual arrangement being subject-verb-object.[4]

Every language employs word order differently. In German, for instance, in certain constructions, one has to wait for the end of the clause to discover what the verb is: "Dog man bites." Word order in Hebrew and Greek can also be very different from English (recall the hopeless example of Young's Literal Translation of John 3:16, found on page 39).

All translations, whether form-driven or meaning-driven, diverge from the word order of the Hebrew or Greek. But meaning-driven translations often do so to a far greater degree in order to produce a natural English that is more readily understood. Consider the following sentences:

A. John did not go on the walk because it rained and was cold.

B. Because it rained and was cold, John did not go on the walk.

Both sentences say the same thing, but sentence A has the more straightforward word order. The main fact—that John missed the walk—is put first, and the reason is put second. Sentence B is an *inverted* sentence: the subordinate information comes first and the main information second. This gives greater emphasis to John's reason for missing the walk, but the reader has to store this information before discovering the real thrust of the sentence.

There is nothing wrong with sentence B. Indeed, in a long narrative sequence the occasional inverted sentence creates variety and holds interest. But some sentences can get very complex, and a lot of information has to be stored before the main point is reached. Generally speaking, the more punctuation a sentence has, the more complex it is. Likewise, words such as *for, which* and *that,* often used to introduce embedded and subordinate clauses, add to the degree of complexity.

Meaning-driven translations shorten sentences and make word order more logical not only to produce a clearer English style but also to make reading (and listening) easier. Word order is especially important when a passage is being read aloud, say in church. While *readers* can go back to the beginning of a sentence and remind themselves of what is written, *listeners* have only one shot at understanding what is said.

The introduction of characters, events and ideas in their logical order, so that readers and hearers are not held in suspense, makes understanding easier. (See, for example, table 2.4 and the choices where the name Mephibosheth should be placed in 2 Samuel 4:4.)

Table 2.4. Two Translations and Word Order in 2 Samuel 4:4

NIV	CEV
Jonathan son of Saul had a son who was lame in both feet. He was five years old when the news about Saul and Jonathan came from Jezreel. His nurse picked him up and fled, but as she hurried to leave, he fell and became crippled. His name was Mephibosheth.	Saul's son Jonathan had a son named Mephibosheth, who had not been able to walk since he was five years old. It happened when someone from Jezreel told his nurse that Saul and Jonathan had died. She hurried off with the boy in her arms, but he fell and injured his legs.

CONNECTIONS

Breaking longer sentences into shorter ones, as many meaning-driven translations do, can create problems, however. As well as producing a flat, monotonous style, the relationship between one part of a sentence and another part of it, or between two sentences, can be lost.

In reviewing the NIV against the more form-driven ESV,[5] Tony Payne highlights the preference of the former for shorter sentences and the removal of many connecting words found in the Greek. One such connecting word is *gar*, occurring 144 times in the Greek text of Romans. The simple dictionary definition of *gar* is "for"; it connects what follows with what has gone before.

The word appears at the beginning of Romans 1:18. The ESV (like the RSV, on which it is based) has "*For* the wrath of God is revealed," thus maintaining the connection with the preceding verses that speak of God's righteousness revealed in the gospel. The NIV does not translate *gar*. In it Romans 1:18 begins, "The wrath of God is being revealed." Of the remaining occurrences of *gar*, the NIV leaves fifty untranslated and renders the rest variously as "for," "because" or "so."

While his point has some validity, Payne overstates his case. Connections between one clause and another or between one sentence and the next often do need to be preserved, but in many instances connecting words in *koinē* (common) Greek carry very little force. And like all other words, their meaning must be determined by context. Sometimes they are better translated in more subtle ways, such as by good English punctuation.

Meanwhile, Payne fails to point out in advocating the ESV over the NIV that both translations insert a paragraph break and a section heading between Romans 1:17 and 1:18, making a complete visual disruption between the two verses—a far more significant factor than the failure to retain the single word *for*.

PRONOUNS

Hebrews 11:4 in the NIV reads: "By faith Abel offered God a better sacrifice than Cain did. By faith he was commended as a righteous man, when God spoke well of his offerings. And by faith he still speaks, even though he is dead." You probably had to read that more than once, because the pronouns are confusing. According to the rules of English grammar, the pronoun *he* in the second sentence should refer back to Cain. Actually Abel is meant. And *he* in the third sentence could also be taken as referring back to God (as being dead!), but once again Abel is intended.

Unlike some form-driven versions, meaning-driven translations generally attempt to employ pronouns in a logical and unconfusing way. They often use a person's name rather than a pronoun in order to make the sense crystal clear. This is particularly important when reading a passage aloud. How much easier would Hebrews 11:4 be if it read: "By faith Abel offered God a better sacrifice than Cain did. By faith Abel was commended as a righteous man when God spoke well of his offerings. And by faith Abel still speaks, even though he is dead"? In fact, the TNIV, a revision of the NIV, does substitute the proper name "Abel" for "he" in the final sentence of this verse.

VERB FORMS AND TENSES

When it comes to verb forms, no two languages employ tenses in exactly the same way. Hebrew, as noted earlier, has only two tenses and is very different from English. Greek, being a European language, is closer to English but still has noticeable differences. Whereas form-driven versions strive to retain the grammatical structures, including the tenses, of the original languages, meaning-driven translations give priority to natural English.

What follows is a "translation" of Mark 1:40-45 that keeps to the tenses employed in the Greek. The basis is the NASB, which marks verbs with an asterisk to indicate the use of the Greek present tense for past action—the so-called historical present. These have been rendered here as present-tense verbs (my italics):

And a leper *comes* to Jesus, beseeching Him and falling on his knees before Him, and *is saying* to him, 'If You are willing, You can cleanse me.' [41]Having been moved with compassion, and having stretched out His hand, Jesus touched him, and *says* to him, 'I am willing; be cleansed.' [42]Immediately the leprosy left him and he was cleansed. [43]And having sternly warned him Jesus immediately sent him away, [44]and *says* to him, 'See that you say nothing to anyone; but go, show yourself to the priest and offer for your cleansing what Moses commanded, as a testimony to them.' [45]But having gone out, he began to proclaim it freely and to spread the news around, to such an extent that Jesus could no longer publicly enter a city, but stayed out in unpopulated areas; and people were coming to Him from everywhere.

Notice the number of verbs in the present tense: "a leper comes," "he says," "is saying" and so forth. This makes the passage sound like a running commentary. Notice too the large number of compound verbs ("having warned," "having gone," "were coming," etc.). While these participial forms are quite natural in Greek, too many produce an unnatural English style.

All translations make some alteration to Hebrew and Greek verb forms when translating into English. If they didn't, the result would be unreadable. But form-driven translations try to make fewer than their meaning-driven counterparts. (One recent but little-known translation that is highly respected for its careful handling of Greek verbs is the International Standard Version; see pp. 196-97.)

MAKING IMPLICIT INFORMATION EXPLICIT

An example of making implicit information explicit can be taken from Luke 18:10, Jesus' introduction to the parable of the Pharisee and the tax collector (see table 2.5). The impact of the parable depends on knowing that Jesus regarded the Pharisees as being full of their own self-importance and that tax collectors were seen as racketeers who had sold their souls to the occupying Romans. One person, the Pharisee, is acting in character; the other, the tax collector, is acting entirely out of character.

Table 2.5. Luke 18:10 in Two Translations

NASB	LB (my italics)
Two men went up into the temple to pray, one a Pharisee and the other a tax collector.	Two men went to the Temple to pray. One was a *proud, self-righteous* Pharisee, and the other a *cheating* tax collector.

Without background knowledge of how Pharisees and tax collectors were regarded, the parable makes little sense. Read enough of the Gospels and one eventually picks up this background information, but the casual reader or newcomer will not be aware of it. The Living Bible, a paraphrase, has thus added a number of descriptive words not in the Greek.

How far it is legitimate to add this extra information is a matter of debate. Too much and translation becomes commentary. All meaning-driven translations make implicit information explicit to some degree; those that do it most are regarded as paraphrases. (A further, more subtle, example of making implicit information explicit appeared in the examination of Ephesians 1:7 on pp. 37-38.)

FIGURES OF SPEECH

A traditional rendering of Psalm 147:10 reads as follows: "His pleasure is not in the strength of the horse, nor his delight in the legs of a man." The CEV translates the same passage as "The Lord doesn't care about the strength of horses or powerful armies."

The Bible uses many figures of speech. Addressing the woman at Jacob's well in Sychar, Jesus spoke of "living water" (Jn 4:10-14). At first, the woman did not understand what he meant and thought he was speaking of running water that could be drawn from a spring that perhaps only he knew about. But Jesus meant the Holy Spirit (see Jn 7:37-39). The powerful metaphor of living water emphasizes the Holy Spirit's power to give life and to refresh the human spirit.

Jesus also used a great number of similes, for example, when speaking about the kingdom of God. Many of his parables, which are really elaborate similes, begin with the words "The kingdom of God is like . . ."

Comparisons include a mustard seed, yeast, treasure and a net, all found
in Matthew 13.

The trouble with figures of speech such as metaphors and similes[6]
is that they are culturally dependent. God makes a wonderful promise
through Isaiah:

> Though your sins are like scarlet,
>   they shall be as white as snow;
> though they are red as crimson,
>   they shall be like wool. (Is 1:18 NIV)

However, this glorious promise makes sense only if we understand
that white indicates purity, and red (the color of blood) indicates the
stain left by the sin of murder. For Westerners, these particular figures
of speech are not too difficult. We are used to the idea that white sym-
bolizes purity—for example, a white wedding dress. But this symbol-
ism is not universal. In parts of the Far East, wedding dresses are traditionally red, not white. Or think of the problems faced by a reader in
a tropical climate where snow is unknown!

Even in the West, as knowledge of the world and language of the
Bible declines, more and more biblical figures of speech are becoming
nonsensical to modern readers. For instance, how readily might today's readers understand Paul's condemnation of the high priest Ana-
nias as a "whitewashed wall"? The metaphor, found in Acts 23:3, is
drawn from the language of Ezekiel 13:10-16, where God compares Israel's false teachers to a wall whitewashed over to hide its flimsy construction and precarious state. Paul is calling his accuser a coward and
a hypocrite.

Jesus used a similar expression when he called the Pharisees "whitewashed tombs," which "look beautiful on the outside but on the inside
are full of the bones of the dead and everything unclean" (Mt 23:27
TNIV). The idea is of something having an attractive exterior but unclean contents. Jesus is emphasizing the Pharisees' hypocrisy.

Other biblical metaphors and similes are drawn from the realms of
agriculture, animal husbandry and fishing, many of which are almost

totally unfamiliar to the typical Westerner. What is the translator to do? Most form-driven versions leave figures of speech intact, putting the onus of interpretation on the reader. However, many meaning-driven translations (and, especially, paraphrases) strive to unpack difficult figures of speech. Using the whitewashed wall of Acts 23:3 as an example, we can see that there are several ways in which this could be done:

- By replacing the figure of speech with a more modern one. "Big hat, no cattle" might be a near (but not exact) modern equivalent. The danger here lies in producing a version that is too colloquial.[7]

- By adding an interpretation while retaining the central picture. Possibilities might be "You are like a wall, finely decorated but flimsily built," or "You are like a wall whose cracks have been painted over." This approach can lead to contrived and cumbersome results. An expression of contempt, such as Paul is trying to make, needs to be short and pointed if it is to carry any real impact.

- By removing the figure of speech altogether and using plain language. In *The Message* (see pp. 182-83), Eugene Peterson goes with "What a fake you are!" The simplified NIV Reader's Version (see p. 174) opts for "You pretender!" God's Word (see pp. 173-74) has simply "You hypocrite!" Of these, perhaps Peterson's makes the best effort in capturing the idea of shallow pretense and lack of substance, but if all figures of speech are removed in the translation process, then a great deal of the Bible's color will be lost. The result can be very flat English.

- By using some sort of explanatory footnote. The CEV does this by explaining that a whitewashed wall is "someone who pretends to be good, but really isn't" and adding a cross-reference to Matthew 23:27-28 (though not to the more significant Ezek 13:10-12). Many study Bibles also add these kinds of explanatory notes.

One particular figure of speech is the euphemism. This is a delicate way of talking about an indelicate subject. To "sleep with" is a euphemism for having sex; to "spend a penny" means (at least to British ears) going to the toilet; and to "pass away" is a polite way of saying someone has died.

The Bible frequently uses euphemisms, and once again the translator must decide whether to retain them in their original form or recast them for the benefit of the target audience. As expected, form-driven versions generally retain euphemisms; meaning-driven translations are more likely to give an interpretive explanation.

When Lazarus died, Jesus told the disciples that his friend had "fallen asleep" (Jn 11:11-14), but they did not understand and had to be told plainly that he was dead. Later, the idea that death was no more to be feared than falling asleep became a very precious concept for believers (cf. Acts 7:60; 1 Cor 11:30; 15:6, 18, 20; 1 Thess 4:13-15). Would it be right to translate it otherwise in these verses?

Some biblical euphemisms divide even the experts. In Ruth 3:7 we are told that the Moabite widow "uncovered the feet" of Boaz. Many evangelical scholars, wanting to think the best of Ruth, take the phrase as it stands and insist that nothing improper happened that night. However, this could well be an account of seduction. If so, Ruth uncovered more than just Boaz's feet! And Ruth's request two verses later that Boaz "spread the corner of his garment" over her was not just a way of asking to be kept warm: it was her way of proposing marriage.

Yet another curious euphemism occurs in 1 Kings 18:27. When Baal fails to respond to the cries of his worshipers, Elijah taunts them. According to the NRSV, he says of Baal, "Either he is meditating, or he has wandered away, or he is on a journey." The middle phrase—"wandered away"—is the one in question. The Living Bible pulls no punches and suggests Baal might be "out sitting on the toilet." The NLT, a revision of the Living Bible, is only a little more discreet with "relieving himself."

APPARENT AMBIGUITIES

In meaning-driven translations the translator chooses between several possible ways of interpreting the raw text, but in a form-driven translation this is left to the reader, preacher or commentator.

An example is the phrase "the love of God." This can be ambiguous, with two or even three meanings: God's love for me, my love for God, or even the love God puts in my heart for others. All three meanings appear in the New Testament. Although phrases like "the love of God" might come across to us as open to interpretation, it is only very rarely that the original writer would have intended them to be at all ambiguous.

In Romans 8:39, in which Paul declares that "nothing can separate us from the love of God that is in Christ" (my translation), it can mean only one thing: God's love for us. But for a question raised in 1 John 3:17—"If anyone . . . sees others in need but has no pity, how can the love of God be in him?" (my translation)—all three meanings are possible. It could refer to the reader's lack of love toward God, or it could be suggesting his heart is closed to God's love—either for himself or for others.

The CEV translates 1 John 3:17 "If we see people in need, we must have pity on that person, or else we cannot say we love God." In contrast, the NLT goes with "How can God's love be in that person?" While the CEV assumes John is talking about our love for God, the NLT understands the verse to mean the love God puts in our hearts for others. Both versions are making an interpretive choice, something unavoidable in any translation but especially so in those that are meaning-driven. A form-driven translation leaves the options open to the reader, while a meaning-driven version will generally opt for just one possible meaning.

The ambiguity of a form-driven translation is advantageous insofar as the reader is aware there is an interpretive choice to be made; it is disadvantageous in that the reader is left to make that choice unaided. If a meaning-driven translation does opt for one possible meaning among several, then the responsibility for making the right choice rests squarely upon the shoulders of the translator. It is an onerous one: the meaning-driven translator must be a very confident exegete.

Gordon Fee, a respected evangelical scholar, generally favors the use of a meaning-driven (or functional equivalence) translation but recognizes the value of comparison with form-driven versions. He writes: "If the best translational theory is functional equivalence, a translation that adheres to formal equivalence is often helpful as a *second* source; it will give you confidence as to what the Greek or Hebrew actually looked like."[8] Elsewhere, however, he discusses his experience of writing two commentaries on 1 Corinthians, the first employing the TEV (strongly meaning-driven) and the second the NIV (moderately meaning-driven):

> Although I tend to favour dynamic equivalence as a translational theory . . . for my own tastes I found far too many absolutely wrong exegetical choices now locked into the biblical text as the reader's only option.[9]

Referring more specifically to the NIV, he says: "As I began to work my way through the text I came to be a bit disillusioned with the NIV and finally secured permission from Zondervan Publishers to alter its text in several places where I found it exegetically impossible."[10]

Using a form-driven translation requires greater effort on the part of the Bible student. But sometimes this can be more rewarding, like the difference between cooking a meal from the raw ingredients and reheating processed food in the microwave. A form-driven translation provides the experienced Bible student with raw ingredients; a meaning-driven version does more of the work but may not always get the cooking exactly right.

Miscellaneous Features of Hebrew and Greek

There are various linguistic features of Hebrew and Greek that are very difficult, even impossible, to translate without the aid of footnotes.

Acrostics. One somewhat contrived feature of Hebrew poetry is the alphabetic acrostic, in which each line begins with a successive letter of the Hebrew alphabet. It is almost impossible to translate an acrostic from one language to another. Most English Bibles simply make an appropriate footnote. The best-known and most elaborate is

Psalm 119. The first eight verses begin with the letter ʾālep; the next eight with the letter bêt, and so on throughout the entire twenty-two letters of the Hebrew alphabet, making 176 (22 × 8) verses in all. Other biblical acrostics are found in Psalms 9—10; 25; 34; 37; 111; 112; 145; Proverbs 31:10-31; and the entire book of Lamentations.

Word play. Many Bible names of people and places have an underlying meaning that forms the basis for a play on words. The account of Jacob and Esau's birth and their fight for the rights of the firstborn (Gen 25:24-34) has several. Jacob means "grasping"; Esau means "hairy"; and Esau's alternative name, Edom, means "red"—hence the red stew exchanged for his birthright.

Judges 15:15-17 records an account of Samson killing heaps of Philistines using just the jawbone of an ass. The words for "ass" and "heap" sound similar. Samson is saying that not only has he created heaps of dead bodies but that he has made asses out of his enemies as well. The place was later called Ramath Lehi: Jawbone Hill.

In the New Testament Jesus makes a clever word play when he compares the Spirit to the wind (in Jn 3:8). The Greek word for Spirit and for wind is the same: *pneuma.*

Once again, as with acrostics, an explanatory footnote may be the translator's best friend.

Alliteration and assonance. "The purpose, pattern and power of prayer" would be a good alliterative title for a talk: all the main words begin with the same letter. There is powerful alliteration in the Hebrew of Isaiah 22:5, which the NIV attempts to capture in English: "The Lord, the Lord Almighty, has a day of *tumult* and *trampling* and *terror.*" The respective Hebrew words are *mĕhûmâ, mĕbûsâ* and *mĕbûkâ.* However, the English translation has been "bent" to keep the alliterative effect: *mĕbûkâ*, translated by the NIV as "terror," is actually closer in meaning to devastation or desolation. A better translation choice that still preserves the alliteration would have been "turmoil."

In fact, this verse provides an example of not only alliteration but assonance—a repeating pattern of vowel sounds. Wisely, the NIV makes no attempt to capture this feature of the original. The NRSV bravely attempts to retain the sense of assonance found in Nahum 2:10: the Hebrew has three consecutive and related words, *bûqâ, měbûqâ* and *měbulāqâ,* which the NRSV renders as "devastation, desolation and destruction!"

Chiasm. Chiasm, meaning crossover, is a device found much more frequently in the Bible than alliteration or assonance. A simple example is in Philemon 5. The RSV retains the Greek word order: "I hear of your love and of the faith which you have toward the Lord Jesus and all the saints." But a Greek reader, spotting the chiasm, would realize Paul was speaking of his readers' love toward the saints (fellow church members) and their faith toward the Lord Jesus. (Figure 2.1 shows how the chiasm works.) The NRSV thus alters the English word order accordingly: "I hear of your love for all the saints and your faith toward the Lord Jesus." So does the NIV, putting faith before love: "I hear about your faith in the Lord Jesus and your love for all the saints."

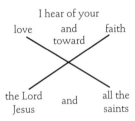

Figure 2.1. Chiasm in Philemon 5

A more extended and slightly different form of chiasm is found in Isaiah 6:10 (ESV, my italics):

Make the *heart* of this people dull,
and their *ears* heavy,
and blind their *eyes*;
lest they see with their *eyes*,
and hear with their *ears*,
and understand with their *hearts*,
and turn and be healed.

Notice the italicized words and the order in which they appear: *heart . . . ears . . . eyes*; then in reverse: *eyes . . . ears . . . hearts*. In the example from Philemon, a meaning-driven translation is preferable to a form-driven one; in the Isaiah example, a form-driven rendering may preserve the chiasm better than a meaning-driven approach.

Other linguistic devices. In more recent years Bible scholars have recognized the importance of various literary devices, particularly those used in biblical narrative. Generally speaking, form-driven translations preserve these features better than meaning-driven renderings. One example is the repetition of key words and phrases. In English, it is not considered good form to repeat a word or phrase, but in Old Testament Hebrew and, to a lesser extent, New Testament Greek, repetition is often used for dramatic effect.

In 2 Samuel 3, the phrase "went in peace" (Hebrew: *wayyēlek bĕšālôm*) is used four times in just three verses. The story then comes to an abrupt end with a similar but contrasting phrase telling us that Joab just "went" (Hebrew: *wayyēlek hālôk*), but certainly not "in peace." The NIV translates verses 21-24 as follows (italics are mine):

> Then Abner said to David, "Let me go at once and assemble all Israel for my lord the king, so that they may make a compact with you, and that you may rule over all that your heart desires." So David sent Abner away, and *he went in peace*.
>
> Just then David's men and Joab returned from a raid and brought with them a great deal of plunder. But Abner was no longer with David in Hebron, because David had sent him away, and *he had gone in peace*. When Joab and all the soldiers with him arrived, he was told that Abner son of Ner had come to the king and that the king had sent him away and that *he had gone in peace*.
>
> So Joab went to the king and said, "What have you done? Look, Abner came to you. Why did you let him go? Now *he is gone!*"

The repetition is apparent to the English reader. But compare the NIV with the REB, which gives priority to English style over the interests of the Hebrew:

Abner said to David, "I shall now go and bring the whole of Israel over to your majesty. They will make a covenant with you, and you will be king over a realm after your own heart." David dismissed Abner, *granting him safe conduct.*

Just then David's men and Joab returned from a raid, bringing a great quantity of plunder with them, and by this time Abner, *having been dismissed,* was no longer with David in Hebron. So when Joab and the whole force were greeted on their arrival with the news that Abner son of Ner had been with the king and *had departed under safe conduct.*

Joab went in to the king and said, "What have you done? You have had Abner here with you. How could you let him go and *get clean away?"*

While the REB brings out the idea of leaving in peace as being granted safe conduct, the literary device is considerably weakened: there is, for instance, no equivalent at all at the end of verse 22 for the Hebrew "gone in peace."[11]

FURTHER FACTORS

Further factors regularly employed by meaning-driven translations, especially common-language translations, to contribute to reading (and listening) ease include

- The use of direct action. "We are forgiven" is easier than "We have forgiveness," and "God forgives us" is easier still. Active sentences are easier than passive: "God loves me" is easier than "I am loved by God." (See also the earlier discussion on Eph 1:7 on pp. 37-39.)

- The use of verbal expressions rather than abstract nouns. "God saves" is easier than "God gives salvation."

- The use of direct rather than indirect speech. "He said, 'I want to go to the market'" is easier than, "He said that he would like to go to the market."

- The use of a variety of sentence lengths to hold interest. Too many very short sentences result in boredom and break up the flow of a passage.

CONCLUSIONS

The characteristics of form-driven and meaning-driven translations can be summarized as follows. The reader must decide whether these are to be regarded as advantages or disadvantages.

Form-driven translations, characteristically,

- are relatively transparent, allowing the reader to see the text in its raw state
- maintain much of the original grammar and sentence structure, showing the author's connections between phrases and sentences
- reveal connections between words and phrases in different passages within the Bible, making them well suited to word studies
- allow ambiguities to be sorted out by readers, preachers or commentators
- reveal the style of the original writers, generally retaining the Bible's own figures of speech and other literary devices
- do not disguise the fact that the Bible is a translation from another time and culture
- often maintain traditional Bible English, usually in the Tyndale/KJV style
- require a high reading ability, a good background knowledge of the Bible and familiarity with the way the Bible's authors originally expressed themselves
- are less likely to become dated than a meaning-driven translation or paraphrase

Form-driven versions are generally better suited to detailed study than to general reading, and to well-established Christians than to new believers or seekers.

Meaning-driven translations typically

- have short, easy sentences and word order
- employ easy vocabulary, especially for theological, cultural and historical terms
- make implicit information explicit

- unpack or replace figurative language
- use various devices to make the Bible easy and interesting to read
- require a generally low reading ability
- avoid ambiguity, opting for only one of several possible meanings
- avoid biblical jargon in favor of a more natural style
- disguise the fact that the Bible is a translated book that originates from a different time and culture

Meaning-driven translations are better suited to reading aloud and general reading than to detailed study, and to new Bible readers than to researchers and students.

Bible translations range from form-driven through meaning-driven to paraphrase. Each can be placed somewhere on the spectrum of literal to free. Making an assessment as to where on that spectrum a particular translation lies is, of necessity, somewhat subjective.[12] Table 2.6 offers my assessment of various versions. Points for and against form-driven and meaning-driven translations have been considered. Taking either translation approach to extremes can produce less than desirable results. A good idea is to regularly use and compare at least one Bible from each camp.

Table 2.6. Bible Versions Organized by Translation Philosophy

Form-driven versions	Meaning-driven versions	Paraphrases
(N)KJV RSV	(T)NIV NJB JB NLT	JBP LB
NASB ESV NRSV	NAB N/REB NCV	GNB CEV *Message*
← More literal		Less literal →

3

A QUESTION OF STYLE

You accepted what we said as the very word of God—which,
of course, it was. And this word continues to work in you who believe.

1 THESSALONIANS 2:13 NLT

⁊

It is a translation's overall style, more than any other feature, that determines our liking for it. Despite being far more accurate than the AV/KJV, the Revised Version of 1885 failed to win over many adherents. Where it departed from the style of the AV/KJV, it did so only for the worse.

A style either attracts or repels. We may find it hard to say exactly what it is about a particular translation style that we like or dislike, but most people have an intuitive feeling for a style that appeals to them. A major factor is familiarity. When considering a new Bible, some will look for one written in a style close to a version they already know and trust. Others go for something radically different: they want an alternative style of translation, perhaps as a means of reinvigorating their Bible reading.

An issue relating to style is reading level. A Bible with too high a reading level is off-putting, but one with too easy or too childish a reading level will quickly create boredom. Several factors impinge on reading level: sentence length and vocabulary being the main ones. But rhythm and flow are also important in creating an overall style. I will look at all of these in this chapter.

STYLE IN THE ORIGINAL

To have all sixty-six books of the Bible together between one set of covers is actually something of a novelty. Until the advent of movable-type printing in the fifteenth century, very few complete Bibles existed.[1] The books of the Hebrew Bible were written on separate scrolls, the medium in which they are still used in Jewish synagogues today. Though the Christian church used scrolls at first, it quickly adopted the codex, or book. Being handwritten, these were very large. Most Christian churches and monasteries had copies of just certain parts of the Bible, typically those sections used for liturgical worship: the Psalms and the Gospels were the most common.

Having a Bible bound in one volume with one consistent translation style means it is all too easy to overlook the great diversity of literature spread across the Bible's sixty-six books. While every Bible translation has its own English style, each book of the Bible has its own distinctive style in the original Hebrew or Greek. There is prose and poetry, narrative and law, the expression of lilting love and of low lament, Gospel and letter, and tedious genealogy and pulsating apocalyptic. Translators have to decide how much to impose their own style and how much to allow the style of the original to come through. While all translations exhibit a particular style to a greater or lesser degree, form-driven translations generally allow more of the style of the individual biblical writers to show through, while meaning-driven versions impose their own distinctive translation style more strongly.[2]

The two factors that a translator can vary the most are vocabulary and sentence structure. These determine a translation's readability. It is to reading level that I now turn before looking at other aspects of translation style.

READING LEVEL

"Reading level" refers to the degree of ease or difficulty a person has in understanding a passage of text set before them. A Bible translation for adults can have either a lower or higher reading level. Some Bibles are specially prepared for children and people for whom English is a second language. Such versions often have a very low reading level.

Reading level is partly dependent on the subject matter and the reader's degree of familiarity with that subject. A small child will not understand a book on astrophysics. This is because the child lacks the necessary reading skills and familiarity with the subject. However, a Supreme Court lawyer may not fare much better with such a book, not because of any deficiency in reading skills but because of a lack of familiarity with the fields of astronomy, physics and mathematics.

Should our imaginary lawyer want to learn about the Big Bang and black holes, she might decide to read up on the subject. But she will probably go for a book written at a popular level, one which explains the concepts of astrophysics in lay terms. The vocabulary, language and style will be as simple as possible. Only later will she progress to books written in an academic or expert style.

Some of the people who want to read the Bible in order to learn about Jesus Christ and the salvation he offers will be young and will not have the reading skills to understand a long word with an abstract meaning, such as *salvation*. Others will be older but will lack familiarity with the history, culture and theological themes of Scripture. Then there will be longstanding Christians for whom phrases like *salvation, redemption* and *kingdom of God* will be rich with precious meaning, and still others who will be theologically trained—professors and pastors for whom words like *justification* and *sanctification* roll easily off the tongue and who understand the differences in nuance between words like *expiation* and *propitiation* (see p. 146).

Of course, when it comes to the reading of Scripture, spiritual insight is as important as human knowledge and understanding. There needs to be an openness to the Spirit of truth, who guides us into all truth (Jn 16:13). But while it is true that "the things that come from the Spirit of God . . . are spiritually discerned" (1 Cor 2:14 NIV), it is still the translator's job to make the Bible text as understandable as possible for his or her target audience. Apart from anything else, this means conveying the meaning of Scripture in the language of today, not yesterday. Paul's desire that his readers "refresh my bowels in the Lord" (Philem 20 AV/KJV) is not a request for colonic irrigation!

But which "language of today" should a translator employ? As already noted, the language understood and appreciated by a well-established Christian is going to be different from the language understood by someone opening a Bible for the first time. While a translator cannot control a Bible reader's familiarity with the subject matter of Scripture, he or she can make a Bible harder or easier to read.

Two principal factors affect the reading level of a translation: sentence construction (length and complexity) and vocabulary selection (the choice of words and phrases). These were already discussed to a certain extent in the previous chapter; I return to them here from the point of view of how they affect a translation's reading level.

Sentence length. Consider Ephesians 1:3-10 in two different, but related, versions. The NIV (1984) translates the passage as follows:

> [3]Praise be to the God and Father of our Lord Jesus Christ, who has blessed us in the heavenly realms with every spiritual blessing in Christ. [4]For he chose us in him before the creation of the world to be holy and blameless in his sight. In love [5]he predestined us to be adopted as his sons through Jesus Christ, in accordance with his pleasure and will—[6]to the praise of his glorious grace, which he has freely given us in the One he loves. [7]In him we have redemption through his blood, the forgiveness of sins, in accordance with the riches of God's grace [8]that he lavished on us with all wisdom and understanding. [9]And he made known to us the mystery of his will according to his good pleasure, which he purposed in Christ, [10]to be put into effect when the times will have reached their fulfillment—to bring all things in heaven and on earth together under one head, even Christ.

The New International Reader's Version (NIrV, 1996; see p. 174) is aimed at younger readers, those for whom English is a second language and those with reading difficulties. Notice how it uses simpler and shorter sentences.

> [3]Give praise to the God and Father of our Lord Jesus Christ. He has blessed us with every spiritual blessing. Those blessings come from the heavenly world. They belong to us because we belong to Christ.
>
> [4]God chose us to belong to Christ before the world was created. [5]So he decided long ago to adopt us as his children. He did it because of what Christ has done. It pleased God to do it. [6]All these things bring praise to his glorious grace. God freely gave us his grace because of the One he loves.
>
> [7]We have been set free because of what Christ has done. Through his blood our sins have been forgiven. We have been set free because God's grace is so rich. [8]He poured his grace on us by giving us great wisdom and understanding.
>
> [9]He showed us the mystery of his plan. It was in keeping with what he wanted to do. It was what he had planned through Christ. [10]It will all come about when history has been completed. God will then bring together all things in heaven and on earth under one rule. The ruler is Christ.

According to one objective readability test (the Flesch-Kincaid test, based on a combination of word and sentence length), the text of Ephesians 1:3-10 in the NIV can be understood only by someone with the reading ability of a college or university student, while the same passage in the NIrV is manageable by someone with the reading ability of an average eight-year-old. Admittedly, the passage is particularly difficult both in content and construction, but bearing in mind that the average reading age of adults is twelve, it is clearly important to make a difficult passage such as this easier to read by the intended target audience. The full results of the Flesch-Kincaid test are set out in table 3.1.

Table 3.1. Readability of Ephesians 1:3-10 in Two Versions, Based on the Flesch-Kincaid Test

	NIV (1984)	NIrV
Total no. of words	164	193
No. of paragraphs	1	4
No. of sentences	5	20
Words per sentence	32.8	9.6
Reading age (school year/grade)	18.2 (13.2)	8.9 (3.9)

However, as well as making a Bible passage too difficult to read, it is also possible to make it too easy. If there are too many short sentences and too many words of just one or two syllables, a competent reader easily gets bored. Most adults find a passage with a reading age of below about nine or ten years (grade 4 or 5) too childish. A fluent or better-educated English speaker would find the NIrV an unsatisfying translation to use for any length of time. Also, the NIrV is some 17.7 percent longer than the NIV: more words have to be read in order to absorb the same information, thus running the risk of losing the reader's interest.

Comparing the same two versions of Ephesians 1, we also observe a simplification of the vocabulary. Some of the substitutions are shown in table 3.2.

Table 3.2. Vocabulary Choices in Two Versions of Ephesians 1:3-10

NIV (1984)	NIrV
heavenly realms	heavenly places
in Christ	belong to Christ
blameless	without blame
predestined	decided long ago
redemption	set free
lavished	poured
reached fulfillment	history completed
head	ruler

Reading-level tests. Most tests for ascertaining the reading level of a book or passage—useful diagnostic tools in grading reading material for classroom use—measure two main factors: sentence length and word length. The results are entered into a formula, and the score that pops out indicates the ease or difficulty a reader will have with the chosen passage.

The Flesch-Kincaid test used above is actually built into the latest versions of Microsoft Word and can do the number-crunching as part of a spell check. The result, expressed as a school grade, is increased by five to yield an actual reading age. For example, a score of 3.7 corresponds to a reading age of 8.7 years (i.e., the average reading ability shown by a child of that age). Most adults read comfortably at a grade level of between 5.5 and 7.0. Lower than this and a text feels too simplistic; above this and reading becomes a strain. A reading grade above 10 is generally achieved only by A-level students, and a grade above 12 only by those with a college or university education.[3]

Table 3.3. Wonderly's Horizons of Difficulty

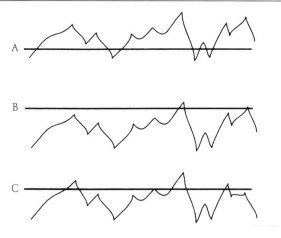

However, most people can read a passage in language that is harder than they would speak or write, provided the level of difficulty is not too great and is not sustained for too long. William Wonderly introduces a helpful concept: the horizon of difficulty.[4] Here a horizontal line represents a person's reading level. In sample A of table 3.3, most of the passage (the complexity of which changes from sentence to sentence) is too difficult and will thwart the reader. In sample B, nearly all of the passage is too simple and will bore the reader. The passage is about right in sample C; the reader is prepared to accept the few peaks of difficulty that exist and work out the meaning of these words or phrases from the surrounding context.

Table 3.4 uses the Flesch-Kincaid test to assess the readability of six Bible passages (Gen 22:1-19; Lev 16:1-22; Ps 40; Jer 10; Lk 15 and Eph 1) in all the major English translations in use today. The most literal (form-driven) are listed at the top, and the table progresses down to the most free (meaning-driven). The six passages were chosen as representative of different kinds of writing in the Bible: narrative (Gen 22), law (Lev 16), poetry (Ps 40), prophecy (Jer 10), storytelling (Lk 15) and letter writing (Eph 1). While tests such as the Flesch-Kincaid take no account of the subject matter of a passage (the ability to *read* the words of a passage is not the same as the ability to *understand* that passage), they do reveal how some biblical genres are harder to read than others. Letters and law codes are typically harder than straight narrative or story.

Surprisingly, poetry is revealed as the easiest genre to read. This, however, is largely due to the fact that Hebrew poetry generally has short sentences. The strong visual imagery and large number of figures of speech employed in Old Testament poetry and prophetic texts can, in reality, make them quite hard to comprehend for those who have little knowledge of the biblical world and culture.

Certain observations can be made:

- Overall, most meaning-based translations have a lower reading level than form-driven ones. And common-language versions have the lowest reading level of all. This is less noticeable in narrative passages but very noticeable in more technical passages such as the Old Testament law codes and the New Testament letters.[5]

- The table verifies another point made in chapters one and two: form-driven translations generally do a better job than meaning-driven ones in allowing the style of the original to show through in the text.

Table 3.4. Flesch-Kincaid Scores for Six Passages of Scripture

Version	Overall	Gen 22	Lev 16	Ps 40	Jer 10	Lk 15	Eph 1	Word count*
NASBu	6.7	6.2	10.4	4.1	4.6	6.4	12+	+3.5
KJV	9.2	7.8	12+	7.2	7.5	7.0	12+	+2.8
NKJV	6.8	6.0	9.6	4.5	5.0	6.5	12+	-1.9
ESV	6.9	6.8	11.4	3.9	4.5	6.5	12+	0.0
NRSV	6.5	6.0	10.3	4.1	4.4	5.8	12+	n/a
NET	6.5	6.0	12+	5.0	4.9	5.9	12+	+5.3
HCSB**	6.3	6.1	10.0	3.4	4.5	5.9	12+	-4.7
NIV	5.9	5.6	9.7	3.1	4.0	5.2	12+	-3.6
NAB	7.2	6.3	10.9	3.7	5.5	6.8	12+	-7.2
NJB	7.4	5.9	12+	4.3	6.2	6.8	12+	-2.0
REB	6.3	5.9	10.2	3.6	5.3	5.2	11.7	-4.7
GW	5.1	5.6	6.7	3.9	4.4	4.9	6.2	-5.6
NCV	5.3	5.3	7.5	3.2	4.5	5.3	7.2	+3.5
ICB	4.0	4.2	4.6	3.0	3.7	4.1	5.1	+7.1
NIrV	3.6	3.6	4.0	2.5	3.8	3.4	4.1	+12.6
NLT (1996)	6.2	5.2	9.0	4.3	4.9	6.5	8.4	+0.7
TEV	5.7	5.7	9.9	4.0	3.9	5.4	8.9	0.0
JBP***	9.1	—	—	—	—	6.8	12+	—
CEV	5.3	5.8	8.1	3.7	4.5	4.8	6.5	-13.6
Message	6.0	4.5	11.4	4.6	5.3	4.8	8.8	-3.4

*Word count = percentage of words more or fewer than the NRSV.
**Scores for the OT passages are based on a pre-publication draft text.
***Only the NT available.

Notice how the meaning-driven translations even out the reading levels across the different genres of writing, whereas the form-driven translations do not.

• Certain versions, notably the CEV, the ICB and the NIrV, have very low reading levels in all genres. This is achieved by breaking longer sentences into two or more shorter sentences. While ideal for children and those with reading difficulties, it can result in a style than adults find wearying.

We are now in a position to create a new chart, one that combines reading ease with degree of literalness (see table 3.5).

Table 3.5. Relative Readability and Literalness in Eighteen Bible Translations

All the above leads into a more general discussion of style. While sentence length and choice of vocabulary can be assessed easily and measured objectively, style, like beauty, is "in the eye of the beholder." However, it does not take long to appreciate that each Bible version has its own style, in some cases a quite distinct one.[6]

FORMAL VERSUS CONVERSATIONAL

It is obvious that some Bible versions are more formal in style than others. More formal versions often retain an older style and give the impression of coming from a previous era. In contrast, English translations that strive for a contemporary feel are often more informal and conversational, and they use the language of everyday speech. Such translations can and do date more easily, like pop music compared with classical.

Examples of Bibles that aim at a more relaxed and conversational style include paraphrases such as the Living Bible (see pp. 151-52), and meaning-driven translations like Today's English Version (pp. 157-58) and the Contemporary English Version (pp. 174-78), all trendsetters in this respect. While some applaud the greater accessibility such a style affords, others fear a dumbing down and a loss of the rich cadences of earlier versions. Further examples of Bibles offering a more conversational style, with an emphasis on natural, everyday English, include the New Century Version (p. 165), God's Word (pp. 173-74) and the New Living Translation (pp. 178-81).

Such translations are often described as "idiomatic," a vague term that can simply mean that a translation falls into the meaning-driven category, or that a deliberate attempt has been made to employ a natural and up-to-date conversational style, one that disguises the fact that the Bible is a translation. Taken too far, however, an idiomatic translation can become an idiosyncratic one, revealing the tastes and temperament of the translator. Nowhere is this more likely than in paraphrases, all of which are one-person translations rather than the work of a committee.

A one-person translation is likely to be more colorful and stylistically distinct than a committee-produced version. The clearest example is that of Eugene Peterson's *The Message* (see pp. 182-83). While there are advantages, not least in encouraging the reading of Scripture through fresh eyes, there can be drawbacks. When style becomes more important than faithful communication of the original, a paraphrase becomes overly interpretive.

But many modern versions, while striving for readable and understandable English, also want to retain a degree of elegance and dignity. Many churches have pew Bibles and will choose a particular translation because it matches their style of worship. Some versions are marked by a somewhat cultured literary style. The New English Bible (see pp. 147-49) is in this "highbrow" category, and its successor (the Revised English Bible, pp. 168-70) only a little less so. Also with distinct—though different—literary styles are some of the Roman Catholic translations, notably the Jerusalem and New Jerusalem Bibles (pp. 153-54, 164-65) and the New American Bible (pp. 154-55). Such translations are often well matched to a more formal church service, especially one employing traditional liturgy.

THE TYNDALE/KING JAMES TRADITION

Some Bible translations stand within the tradition of the AV/KJV as revisions (or even revisions of revisions of revisions). They display a family likeness and to a certain extent have a shared style.

Often readers complain when alterations are made to their most treasured verses, thus even translations claiming to be independent of the AV/KJV family sometimes reveal their indebtedness to it. For instance, in certain well-known passages such as the Lord's Prayer and Psalm 23, the NIV and other translations show a familiarity with the phrasing and cadences of the 1611 version.

Much of the genius of the AV/KJV is due to the work of William Tyndale (see pp. 118-121), whose translation of the New Testament and parts of the Old Testament underlie it. As noted above (p. 45), he employed short words and pithy vocabulary to full effect. And he had the ability to put them together in a wonderful way that accounts for the rhythmic quality of the AV/KJV. The following modern translations all stand within the Tyndale/ King James tradition: RSV, NASB, NKJV, NRSV and ESV (the diagram on p. 193 shows how they are related). All are classed as form-driven versions.

Thee/thou language. A notable feature of the AV/KJV is its archaic language. Beyond the choice of vocabulary, it includes "thees and thous" and verbs ending in "eth" and "est."

Modern translations, even those within the AV/KJV tradition, have mostly dropped any semblance of thee/thou language. Three versions (the RSV, the NEB and the original edition of the NASB) maintain thee/thou language only for passages addressing God in prayer. The original Hebrew and Greek, however, did not use special language for addressing God. There is no good reason to choose a Bible with this kind of archaic language. The three translations mentioned have all been superseded by better revisions—the NRSV and ESV, the REB and the NASBu respectively.[7]

BIBLE ENGLISH

Form-driven translation attempts to keep to the language forms of the original as far as possible. This includes grammatical structures, word order and vocabulary. Often what results is not entirely natural English, but something we might term *biblish*. Certain time-honored phrases come immediately to mind: "And it came to pass"; "Truly, truly, I say unto you"; "Thus saith the Lord"; and so on. Such phrases may be precious and entirely understandable to a believer steeped in the Bible for decades, but they will strike others as being something other than the English of everyday use. And a figurative phrase like "my cup overflows" (Ps 23:5 NIV) may not be understood at all (see p. 43).

Another example of biblish comes in the common form of translation of John 3:16: "For God so loved the world that he gave his only Son." Ask almost anyone to put this into their own words and they will say, "For God loved the world *so much* that . . ." This is not, however, what the verse means. Here "so" (Greek *houtōs*) means "thus" or "in this way," not "so much." A better translation would be: "For this is how God loved the world: he gave his only Son." But most translators prefer to stick with the familiar wording. Form-driven versions, especially, can be reluctant to move away from the traditional phrasing in passages that are well known to readers.

Biblish can come in more subtle forms too. Matthew 4:4 in the NRSV reads: "One does not live by bread alone." The older RSV had "Man shall not live by bread alone." The NRSV is an improvement in two respects: "Man" is replaced by the more inclusive "one" (notwithstanding its more formal tone); and the archaic "shall not" is replaced by the more modern and natural "does not." However, we still have an oddity: "live *by* bread." People might live *by* hard work, but they do not live *by* bread—people live *on* bread. But examples like this are not always spotted, especially by those well used to Bible English.

One further example will again demonstrate the difference between form-driven and meaning-driven translations. In John 15:9, Jesus gives his disciples a command: "Remain in my love." This is how the Greek is translated by the NIV and the NLT. The NRSV, ESV and NASB follow the AV/KJV and have the very similar "Abide in my love."

Perhaps surprisingly, the creators of the CEV say this was the most difficult phrase to translate meaningfully in the entirety of their translation project.[8] As rendered in most form-driven translations, it is not natural English. What does it mean to remain in someone's love? A husband going off to fight a war does not say to the wife he is leaving behind, "Now remain in my love, won't you, darling?" The Greek carries a two-way meaning: we should continually remember a person's love for us *and* we should maintain our love for them. The CEV captures the reciprocal nature of Jesus' command in its translation: "Remain faithful to my love for you."

COLLOQUIALISM AND DIALECT

Some more idiosyncratic translations and paraphrases employ colloquialisms and slang. Others are written in a particular regional dialect. Recent paraphrases of parts of the Bible have been prepared in a Yorkshire dialect, in Cockney rhyming slang, in limerick verse and even in Australian twang—more for amusement, however, than as serious translation attempts. Yorkshireman David Hallamshire renders Goliath's challenge to the Israelites (1 Sam 17:9-10) thus:

"Nar then! Does tha need a whole army to settle this or what luv," he says and he were struttin up and darn like a bantam cock he were. "I'll be bloke what fights for Philistines, and tha can choose someone to fight for yorn piddlin lot, and we can settle it reet here and nar wi' just two on us."[9]

Colloquialisms and slang are best avoided in Bible translation. They are not universally understood and can become dated very quickly. For example, in the late 1990s it was common among young people to describe a good experience as "wicked," as in, "That rollercoaster ride was wicked." Yet imagine Jesus saying, "I am the well wicked shepherd"!

VERBOSITY

Many meaning-driven and easy-to-read versions tend toward wordiness. As already noted, the NIrV has a 17.7 percent higher word count than the NIV in Ephesians 1:3-10, and a 16.8 percent higher word count across the Bible as a whole. Generally speaking, a hard-hitting and expressive style is achieved by using fewer words, not more. The CEV, one of the few meaning-driven translations to buck this trend toward verbosity, is some 13 percent shorter than other Bibles, though this is in large part due to the way it conflates the lines of Hebrew poetry and recasts figurative language.

READING ALOUD

Some Bibles, in aiming at literalness and accuracy, do not read aloud well. This is true, for example, of the New American Standard Bible (pp. 156-57), which is a good Bible for study but which cannot be recommended for church use. Others, because they employ everyday English, lack a certain dignity when read aloud. This is particularly noticeable in a church tradition that employs well-crafted liturgy. But there are many versions where the translators have deliberately striven for a style that is well suited to public reading.

The AV/KJV was "appointed to be read in churches": its prime purpose was liturgical. But many translations of the twentieth century had other purposes: detailed study on the one hand or evangelism on the other. Thankfully, there has been a trend back toward Bibles that read well. The final wording of the Contemporary English Version (pp. 174-78) was not approved until every passage had been heard read aloud.

To make its sentences flow, the translators did not permit more than three consecutive unaccented syllables. Note, for example, how hard it is to read aloud the following two sentences, taken from other translations:[10] "You yourselves admit, then, that you agree with what your ancestors did" (Lk 11:48); "For it was better with me then than now" (Hos 2:7). The CEV renders them "You must think that was the right thing for your people to do" and "Life was better then" respectively.

I have already noted the value of having sentences that introduce people, events and ideas in a natural and logical order. This is particularly important when the Bible is heard rather than read. If confused or uncertain about the connection between parts of a sentence or paragraph, readers can cast their eyes back up the page. But the listeners have no such luxury; a passage must make sense on first hearing.

A good public reader will help the listener by placing pauses in the right place, but the translator has to remember that punctuation is silent. Read aloud from the RSV, Luke 22:35 could easily be misunderstood: "And he said to them: 'When I sent you out with no purse or bag or sandals, did you lack anything?' They said, 'Nothing.'" The hearer might easily think Jesus' disciples *said nothing* rather than saying, "Nothing." In the NRSV the final sentence has been altered: "They said, 'No, not a thing.'"

The LORD. One particular word that translators struggle over is the name given to God in the Old Testament. The Hebrew word, without vowels, is YHWH. Known as the *tetragrammaton* ("the four letters"), it is generally pronounced *yahweh*. The meaning of *yahweh* is given in Exodus 3, the account of God's meeting with Moses at the burning bush. It means "I am" or "I will be," emphasizing the eternal and wholly independent nature of God. Because the Jews believed it blasphemous to utter God's name aloud, they substituted *'adōnāy* ("my master") when reading out loud, a practice still followed today by any student of Hebrew.

The ASB of 1901 employed "Jehovah" for YHWH, and in some other versions the name Jehovah is occasionally found as a way of translating YHWH when it forms part of a combination name, for example Jehovah-jireh (in Gen 22:14, meaning "the Lord my Provider") and Jehovah-shalom (Judg 6:24, "the Lord our Peace"). But in most translations "LORD" is used, the small capitals indicating that the divine name is intended.

Two versions that render YHWH as Yahweh are the Jerusalem Bible (1966) and its revision, the New Jerusalem Bible (1985), but the preface of the former suggests that those reading aloud might want to substitute "the Lord" for "Yahweh."

MEMORABILITY

A related feature of translations that are easy to read aloud is that they are generally easy to memorize. Many people know verses as they learned them from the AV/KJV in childhood, even though they have long since moved on to more modern translations.

Further features of vocabulary and style will be dealt with in part two under the consideration of individual translations. Next, however, we must take a brief look at the translation of biblical poetry, where style is of even more critical importance.

HEBREW POETRY

If style is important in translating prose, it is even more important in translating poetry. Close to one third of the Old Testament is poetry, predominantly in the Psalms, together with the books of wisdom and prophecy. There is even a smattering within the narrative books: Moses and Miriam's songs in Exodus 15 and Deborah's in Judges 5 are counted among the oldest parts of the Bible.

The presence of poetry in the Old Testament was not recognized in early English translations. The RV (1885) and ASV (1901) were the first major translations to use indented lines to indicate Hebrew poetry, though neither were as thorough in doing so as the later RSV (1952) and subsequent translations.

Poetry represents an elevated style of writing. In English and other languages, it is generally marked out by two main features: rhythm and rhyme. While Hebrew poetry has rhythm, it does not rhyme. Instead, it employs a device called *parallelism*. We can think of parallelism as being rhyming ideas. There are three basic kinds (all examples are from the ESV):

1. Repeating (or synonymous) parallelism, in which the second line echoes or reinforces the first:

    > I know that the Lord will maintain the cause of the afflicted,
    >   and will execute justice for the needy. (Ps 140:12)

2. Progressive (or synthetic) parallelism, in which the second line builds on the first:

    > My days are swifter than a weaver's shuttle
    >   and come to their end without hope. (Job 7:6)

3. Opposing (or antithetical) parallelism, in which the second line contrasts with the first:

    > Better is a poor man who walks in his integrity
    >   than a rich man who is crooked in his ways. (Prov 28:6)

Perhaps it is in God's good providence that the poetry of the Bible is constructed in this way. Because it depends on rhyming ideas, Hebrew parallelism is relatively easy to translate into other languages, whereas maintaining rhyming words and line endings would pose an almost impossible challenge for a translator. However, Hebrew parallelism—particularly when it becomes repetitive—is not a natural form of English. Also, poetry deploys a great deal of visual imagery and a large number of figures of speech, many of which are not readily understandable to the modern English reader (see above, pp. 55-58). For these two reasons, while form-driven translations generally preserve the forms of biblical poetry when translating into English, some meaning-driven versions sometimes do not. Table 3.6 compares two translations of Psalm 18:13-15.

While the NRSV closely follows the form of the Hebrew, the CEV makes considerable changes. The parallelism, clearly seen in the NRSV, is all but lost in the CEV. The first two lines have been conflated into one, as have two further lines in the second verse: "You scattered your enemies with arrows of lightning." The phrase "at your rebuke" is

Table 3.6. Psalm 18:13-15 in Two Translations

NRSV	CEV
The LORD also thundered in the heavens and the Most High uttered his voice. And he sent out his arrows, and scattered them; he flashed forth lightnings, and routed them. Then the channels of the sea were seen, and the foundations of the world were laid bare at your rebuke, O LORD, at the blast of the breath of your nostrils.	LORD Most High, your voice thundered from the heavens, as hailstones and fiery coals poured down like rain. You scattered your enemies with arrows of lightning. You roared at the sea, and its deepest channels could be seen. You snorted, and the earth shook to its foundations.

moved up two lines in the CEV and becomes "You roared at the sea."

The CEV is to be commended for its brevity and clarity, but has it lost too much and departed too far from a literal translation? From where did the translators get the phrase "poured down like rain" in the second line? And can we be sure the CEV is right in interpreting the NRSV's "them" as King David's enemies?

Again, we are back to the question of whether the translator should attempt to make the text accessible to the reader at the risk of being too interpretive, or whether the translator should give a raw translation and leave interpretation up to the reader. To a large extent, it will depend on the translator's intended audience. Many Christians will find value in having access to both kinds of translation: form-driven and meaning-led.

One translation that has attempted to translate the poetry of the Bible into genuinely English metrical poetry, complete with rhyming lines, is the ISV. See pages 196-97 for a discussion of this and examples of its poetry.

THE UNITY OF SCRIPTURE

As has already been noted, each book of the Bible has a distinct genre and style. And each author uses words in a particular way with particular meanings. It makes sense, therefore, to translate each book as though it stood alone.

But there are two difficulties with this, the first practical and the second theological. First, later biblical writers often draw on earlier writings. Most obvious is the large number of Old Testament quotations in the New Testament, along with its hundreds of allusions to Old Testament ideas and patterns of thought.

There are also places in the Bible where it looks as though one writer has copied from another. Within the Synoptic Gospels (Matthew, Mark and Luke) are many parallel, almost identical passages.[11] There are also close parallels between parts of Kings and Chronicles, and some Psalms are repeated. These quotations, allusions and parallel passages give Scripture a *practical* unity. But the Bible also has a *theological* unity. The whole of Scripture is God-breathed (2 Tim 3:16), and the grand, unifying theme of Scripture is Christ.

This practical and theological unity raises issues for the translator. Form-driven translations, where possible, try to render parallel passages with the same wording in both passages. Where, in a team effort, different translators are working on different books of the Bible, it may be necessary for a supervising editor to bring the translation of parallel passages into line. This can be quite a challenge, especially in the Synoptic Gospels, where there are parallels between not just two but often all three writers. There are also some triple parallels in the Old Testament, most notably the parallels of 2 Kings 18—20 in 2 Chronicles 32 and Isaiah 36—39.

Old Testament quotations in the New Testament are particularly tricky because the New Testament writers generally quote the Greek translation of the Old Testament, known as the Septuagint (see pp. 207-8), rather than the original Hebrew. Translators generally do not try to harmonize the two; thus the wording is not entirely identical.

An area where translators differ is over the translation of Old Testament passages that New Testament writers saw as being messianic. Table 3.7 shows how the NRSV and NIV differ in their use of capitalization in Psalm 2:2.

Table 3.7. Capitalization in Two Versions of Psalm 2:2

NRSV	NIV
The kings of the earth set themselves, and the rulers take counsel together, against the Lord and his anointed . . .	The kings of the earth take their stand and the rulers gather together against the Lord and against his Anointed One.

Originally the reference to God's anointed (Hebrew *māšiah*) was to the king of Israel, but in Acts 4:26, where Psalm 2 is quoted, it is taken to refer to Christ as Messiah. Is the NIV right to read this messianic reference back into Psalm 2 by its use of capital letters for "Anointed One"? Or is the NRSV right in allowing readers to decide for themselves how the psalm is to be interpreted? In Psalm 2:6-7 the NIV also capitalizes "my King" and "my Son." Table 11.3 (p. 190) offers further examples of the use of capitalization to highlight messianic references.

A further problem occurs in Psalm 2:12, where the Hebrew is unclear. The AV/KJV has "kiss the Son." Many evangelical translations (such as the NIV, the NASB and the ESV) follow suit, preferring to maintain this apparent messianic reference. Other, more ecumenical translations, such as the RSV and NRSV, accept a widely held scholarly amendment and render the phrase "kiss his feet."

Isaiah 7:14. In discussing messianic references, no verse has proved more controversial than Isaiah 7:14. Isaiah was referring to a child who would be born by natural means in his own day, probably within the royal household. The significant Hebrew word is ʿalmâ, a word meaning any unmarried young woman—not necessarily a virgin. The Greek Septuagint, however, translated ʿalmâ by *parthenos*, a word carrying the narrower technical sense of "virgin." It is the Septuagint that is quoted in Matthew 1:23 and is said to be fulfilled in Mary's virginal conception of Jesus.

The RSV was bitterly attacked and copies publicly burned when it translated Isaiah 7:14 "a young woman shall conceive" instead of the traditional "a virgin shall conceive" (see pp. 145-46). Translations that are more theologically conservative retain "virgin." While this preserves the unity of Scripture, such translations are left open to the accusation of bias and of reading back into the Old Testament truths that are revealed in their fullness only in the New Testament.

Table 3.8 indicates how some major translations deal with Isaiah 7:14. Some offer explanatory footnotes; others do not. Three Roman Catholic translations are given at the bottom.

Table 3.8. Isaiah 7:14 in Various Translations

Version	Text	Footnote (if any), with italics as used by each version
KJV	virgin	—
NASB	virgin	or maiden
TEV	young woman	The use of "virgin" in Matt. 1.23 reflects a Greek translation of the Old Testament.
N/REB	young woman	—
RSV	young woman	or *virgin*
NRSV	young woman	Gk *the virgin*
ESV	virgin	—
NIV	virgin	—
NLT	virgin	or *young woman*
CEV	virgin	or "young woman"
NKJV	virgin	—
JB	maiden	The Greek version reads "the virgin."
NJB	young woman	Gk reads "the virgin."
NAB	virgin	—

VISUAL STYLE

Three additional features of certain translations may have a bearing on their desirability. Other visual features are dealt with at the end of chapter five.

Punctuation. Older translations often began a new line for every new verse.[12] Most modern translations lay down the text in paragraphs, which is much preferable. One translation, the NASBu, is available in either option. A good Bible will also print poetry as poetry, with indented lines; a few do not.

Older versions, including the AV/KJV, do not use quotation marks for direct speech. Thankfully, all modern translations follow standard English practice in doing so.

Capital letters. Another habit, found only in a few relatively recent translations, is the use of capital letters for pronouns referring to God: *He, His, You, Your* and so on. The Amplified Bible, NASBu, NKJV and HCSB follow this unhappy convention. As well as being contrary to the rules of English punctuation, it can mislead the eye, which expects capital letters to signal the start of a new sentence. Both Hebrew and early Greek had only one set of letters, not separate uppercase and lowercase alphabets, and thus would not call for this trend. And, of course, when read aloud, such capitalization makes no difference to the listener.

One place where most Bibles usefully employ a capital letter is for *Spirit* when the word refers to the Holy Spirit as opposed to the human spirit. However, Bible students should be aware that this too is a matter of interpretation: sometimes it is not easy to determine whether God's Spirit or the human spirit is intended. For example, in Romans 1:4, is it the Holy Spirit or Jesus' human spirit that Paul is writing about? The NRSV refers to the "spirit of holiness" but offers "Spirit" as an alternative in the footnotes. The NIV and NASBu reverse this, putting "Spirit" in the text and "spirit" in the footnotes.[13]

The use of capital letters to indicate Old Testament phrases taken as having messianic significance was discussed on pages 86-87.

Italics. Certain translations (mostly form-driven) employ an italic typeface or other devices to indicate words that have been supplied in English in order to make sense of the text. Versions that use italics in this way include the AV/KJV, the NKJV, the NASB and the NASBu. Such a device can be misleading: in modern English, italics imply emphasis and are reserved for words of greater, not lesser, importance. Nor can italics be "heard" when read aloud.

The JB and NJB employ italics to indicate an Old Testament quotation in the New Testament. As always, reading a Bible's introduction will explain its unique features.

Much more could be said about style, both linguistic and visual, but enough has been said to give the Bible-buyer and reader a good idea what to look for when considering a particular translation or edition. The next chapter addresses another troublesome linguistic feature with which today's translator must wrestle: gender.

4

HIS AND HERS

GENDER ACCURACY

One does not live by bread alone,
but by every word that comes from the mouth of God.

MATTHEW 4:4 NRSV

⌒

Early editions of the Authorized (King James) Version were divided into "He" and "She" Bibles. The difference lay in the translation of just one verse: Ruth 3:15. While the first printing of the AV/KJV in 1611 asserted that "*he* [Boaz] went into the city [of Bethlehem]," the second and third printings made later that year stated that "*she* [Ruth] went into the city."

Neither rendering can be said with absolute certainty to be the right one: the Hebrew manuscripts themselves are divided, and several modern translations have a footnote to alert readers to this minor variance.

On a far greater scale, however, and affecting almost every page of the Bible is the issue of gender and the language we employ to describe men and women. A concern for political correctness has changed the very way we use the English language. We are no longer comfortable referring to a woman who presides over a meeting as its *chairman*: she is rather its *chairwoman, chairperson* or just *chair*.

As recently as twenty or even fifteen years ago, no one would have had a problem with the statement found in Romans 3:28 (NIV): "We maintain that a man is justified by faith." It was generally understood and accepted that in this context *man* was a generic term including both male and female.

During the 1980s and early 1990s, what was meant may have been understood but was becoming increasingly unacceptable, even offensive. Today, the use of *man* to include both men and women is not only widely offensive, it is often not understood. Some today might understand the NIV's wording as referring only to men and apparently excluding women. A younger person or someone unacquainted with biblical language who read that "a *man* is justified by faith" might raise what seems to them an obvious question: "By what then is a *woman* justified?"

New Testament professor Mark Strauss writes:

> A new controversy has emerged in the field of Bible translation. The issue concerns what are being called "gender-inclusive" Bible versions. If the early stages of this debate are any indication, it promises to be more complex, more confusing and more divisive than any translation controversy in history.[1]

Such a statement sounds strange to my British ears, but Strauss is writing from an American perspective. In the spring of 1997 an almighty row broke out when it was learned that a new, inclusive-language edition of the NIV (the NIVi) had been prepared for publication. Although not the first to adopt inclusive language, it was the first to excite such a furor, for as Mark Strauss explains, "the popularity of the NIV among evangelicals has made [its revision] a lightning rod of controversy."[2]

Opposition from conservative Christians who saw a feminist and unisex conspiracy behind this new edition resulted in an about-face on the part of the International Bible Society (IBS) who hold the NIV copyright. The NIVi went unpublished in the United States, though publication did go ahead in Britain.

The IBS promised not to change the wording of the original NIV but five years later went ahead with the publication of Today's New International Version (TNIV), incorporating what they call "gender-accurate" language (see pp. 182-86 for more of the story). The NIV and the TNIV are now in print parallel to each other, and in Britain the NIVi remains available as well.

In the NIVi and TNIV, Romans 3:28 is rewritten: "We maintain that a person is justified by faith." Who could doubt that this is a perfectly acceptable translation? And if it is better understood by a majority of English speakers, then we must conclude that it is also a more accurate translation.

But introducing inclusive language into an English translation of the Bible is far from easy. Accuracy has to be maintained: did the original author intend men and women to be understood, or just men, or just women? And good style has to be kept; thankfully no inclusive-language version has opted for the "he or she, his or her" approach of the office memorandum.

WORKMEN OR WORKERS?

There is, in the English employed in traditional translations, a small number of male-oriented words. These are generally easy to change without controversy:

- workmen = workers
- craftsmen = craft workers or skilled workers
- herdsmen = herders
- foremen = slave-drivers
- kinsmen = relatives
- fellow countrymen = kindred
- watchmen = guards or lookouts
- bowmen = archers
- horsemen = riders

Of course, there is no need to make these changes when it is clear that only men are in mind. For example, when horsemen are part of an army they are unlikely to be female, so the change to "riders" is unnecessary.

FATHERS OR ANCESTORS?

Particularly in the Old Testament there is a large number of references to ancestors and descendants. And because ancient Israel was a patriarchal society (a cultural fact that should not be disguised), the family tree is mostly traced through the male line.

Where "father" means male parent (as in "David was the father of Solomon"), there is no reason to make any alteration, but where "fathers" or "forefathers" means "ancestors," then arguably that is the better term.

CHILDREN OF ISRAEL?

Likewise, "son" can refer to a particular person (e.g., "Jonathan, son of Saul"), or it can refer to more distant descendants. A common Hebrew phrase, *běnê-yiśrāʾēl*, refers to the people—both male and female—belonging to the Israelite nation. "Children of Israel," "people of Israel" or just "Israelites" are acceptable alternatives, but a literal, dictionary-definition translation is *"sons* of Israel." The very literal NASB does indeed have "sons of Israel" throughout the Old Testament even though the older AV/KJV uses "children of Israel."[3] Gender-inclusive language is not entirely new!

A particular case where most agree that "son" should be retained is in the messianic title "Son of Man." Jesus frequently referred to himself in this way, the origin of the title stemming from Daniel's vision of "one like a son of man" in Daniel 7:13. How the phrase should be translated elsewhere in the Old Testament is open to debate; for instance, Psalm 8:4 has provoked particular controversy: "What is man that you are mindful of him, or the son of man that you care for him?" (NIV).

BROTHERS AND SISTERS?

In the New Testament letters, readers are often addressed as *adelphoi*, traditionally translated "brothers." As Paul and other writers intended their letters to be read by the whole church, both men and women are clearly in view. Inclusive translations, therefore, have "brothers and sisters."

While acknowledging this, the English Standard Version (see pp. 187-92), a version opposed to all but a minimal use of inclusive language, has just "brothers" but offers an unwieldy footnote to the effect that "the plural Greek word *adelphoi* . . . refers to siblings in a family. In New Testament usage, depending on the context, *adelphoi* may refer either to men or to both men and women who are siblings (brothers and sisters) in God's family, the church."[4]

The NRSV, very thoroughgoing in its use of inclusive language, consistently has "brothers and sisters" in the text but has a somewhat counterproductive footnote indicating that the Greek says "brothers." The Greek does not say "brothers"; it says *adelphoi*. The question for all translators is, what does *adelphoi* mean? While the standard dictionary definition may be "brothers," the meaning in context is "brothers and sisters."[5]

MAN

Greek and Hebrew each use two words for "man." The Hebrew 'ādām and the corresponding Greek *anthrōpos* are generally used in an inclusive sense: that is, they usually refer to human beings collectively, not just males. In contrast, the Hebrew 'îš and the corresponding Greek *anēr* usually refer specifically to the male of the species. With both pairs of words, however, the important qualifier is *usually*: incidents could be cited where 'ādām and *anthrōpos* refer exclusively to males and several more where 'îš and *anēr* refer to people in general.

Opponents of the NIVi devised what are called the Colorado Springs guidelines, named after the place where they were written. These guidelines stipulate that " 'îš should ordinarily be translated 'man' and 'men' and Greek *anēr* should almost always be so translated."[6] The ESV, a revision of the RSV, follows these guidelines closely, as does the HCSB. But it is the context that needs to be the determining factor. Those who adhere to the principles of form-driven translation will invariably come unstuck if they simply follow the dictionary definition of these Hebrew and Greek words. For instance, in James 1:7-8, the two Greek words for "man" are used interchangeably: "That man (Greek *anthrōpos*) should not think he will receive anything from the Lord; he is a double-minded man (Greek *anēr*), unstable in all he does." The same problem is found in James 1:12, 20, 23; 3:2. In every incident, James employs *anēr* in a nonstandard way to refer to people generally, not just men. Similarly, there are verses in the parallelism of Old Testament poetry where the Hebrew words *'ādām* and *'iš* are used interchangeably. Examples include Job 25:6; Psalms 8:4; 90:3; Isaiah 51:12; 56:2.

The only sensible course of action is to translate on a case-by-case basis. In order to translate accurately, the translator must constantly ask the question, did the writer, when referring to men, intend to include women as well? Or was he thinking purely of the male of the species? In some cases it is hard to tell. For instance, in Exodus 33:8, 10, was it all the people or just the menfolk who stood at their tent doors when Moses entered the tabernacle? It is not clear. For further examples and discussion, see *Distorting Scripture?* by Mark Strauss and *The Inclusive Language Debate* by Don Carson.

It should be noted that in many cases the word *man* does not translate any particular Greek or Hebrew word at all; that is to say, it has been supplied to make sense in English but is not there in the original. In such cases, there is little justification for retaining "man" in translation. If singular, "someone" would be an acceptable substitute; if plural, then "people" would be a good translation.

A related issue is how we should translate *man* when the whole human race is in view. The Colorado Springs Guidelines state that the human race should ordinarily be designated by the word *man*. But should it? In Genesis 1:26, God says, "Let us make man *('ādām)* in our image." The story goes on to tell of the creation of Adam *and* Eve, who together and jointly embody the image of God. While the NIV retains "man," the NIVi has "human beings," and the NRSV "humankind," a neologism some would regard as contrived. The NLT has "people," while the CEV goes for "humans."

HE OR SHE, HIM OR HER, HIS OR HERS?

The greatest difficulty for translators, however, comes in dealing with personal pronouns and adjectives. In English, first-person pronouns and adjectives *(I, we, me, us, our, ours)* are gender free; likewise the second person, both singular and plural *(you, your, yours)* and the third-person plural *(they, them, their, theirs)*. But third-person singular pronouns are gender specific *(he, she, him, her, his, hers)*. This raises problems in translating sentences such as Proverbs 16:9, given here in five versions:

RSV   A man's mind plans his way, but the LORD directs his steps.

NCV   People may make plans in their minds, but the LORD decides what they will do.

NLT   We can make our plans, but the LORD determines our steps.

NIV   In your heart you may plan your course, but the LORD determines your steps.

NRSV   The human mind plans the way, but the LORD directs the steps.

The form-driven RSV, produced before there was a concern over inclusive language, is entirely male-oriented: "A *man's* mind . . . *his* way . . . *his* steps." The NCV opts for the plural. This is the most common approach to avoiding male pronouns in the singular, but perhaps the least satisfactory. Pluralizing sentence after sentence not only flattens the style of a translation, but also compromises the personal application of God's Word and inevitably makes a translation less literal in its rendering.

While the NLT takes the less usual route of changing third-person references into first-person ones (and plural at that), the NIVi goes for the second person; but is the writer now addressing one person or more than one? Is something of the individuality lost? The NRSV makes the verse into a universal principle—ideally suited to the book of Proverbs—but "the way . . . the steps" reads awkwardly.

Another device, often used by the NRSV (though not in this instance), is to employ the pronouns *one* or *anyone*, the only third-person singular pronouns in English that are not gender specific. This works grammatically—the third-person singular is retained—but sounds as if the Queen were speaking: "One's mind plans one's way, but the LORD directs one's steps." An alternative is to retain the third-person singular but then to use *they/their/theirs* as though they were singular pronouns: "A person plans their way, but the LORD directs their steps." While this practice is now common in spoken English, some regard it as unsuitable for written English, especially in a formal text such as the Bible.

So, should Bibles employ inclusive language or not? Before that question can be answered, we need to understand the issues involved a little better.

INCLUSIVE LANGUAGE AND GENDER ACCURACY

Producing a faithful Bible translation should have nothing to do with any social or political agenda. We discover what we are to believe from God's Word; we do not impose our beliefs on it or on the way it is translated. Nor can we pretend that the Bible was written against anything other than a male-oriented cultural background. However, it is the translator's task to convey the original meaning of Scripture to a contemporary audience. So if language changes, then it is necessary to change the way we translate. We do this in all other aspects of the English language, so why not gender?

According to James 5:11, "the Lord is very *pitiful*." That is how, nearly four hundred years ago, the translators of the AV/KJV rendered the wonderful-sounding Greek word *polysplanchnos*. At the time it was a perfectly correct rendering, but today it would be both misleading and inaccurate to translate it as "pitiful." Today *pitiful* means "wretched" or "pathetic," not "full of pity" as it once did. Most modern versions go with "full of compassion" (NIV) or something similar. If it is necessary to update a Bible translation when words like *pitiful* change their meaning, isn't it equally necessary to update a translation when far more common words like *man, brother* and even *he* change their meaning?

GOD TALK

A few translations have gone even further and have attempted to change the language relating to God. *The Inclusive New Testament* (1994, published in America by Priests for Equality) and *The New Testament and Psalms: An Inclusive Version* (1995, published in the USA by Oxford University Press) use the NRSV as their starting point (see pp. 172-73), and remove masculine pronouns and other language forms relating to God. "Father" becomes "Father-Mother" or "Parent." "God" is no longer "King" but "Ruler" or "Sovereign." And Jesus becomes "God's Child," not "God's Son." The Holy Spirit is portrayed as female.

In some cases, the author's intended meaning has been deliberately altered. Marriages in which wives respect or submit to their husbands become "partnerships of mutual respect," and there are many other similar alterations on the basis of political correctness and a strongly feminist agenda. Strauss states the case well when he sets the limits for inclusive language:

> If (and only if) a gender-inclusive rendering more accurately reflects the author's intended meaning, then that translation should be adopted. If a large percentage of contemporary readers have the impression of being excluded by generic masculine terms, then those terms are inaccurate and should be revised in ways that convey more precisely the author's intention of inclusion. This is not "re-writing the Bible," as some have suggested; it is more accurately translating the sense intended by the Holy Spirit.[7]

Those favoring form-driven translations tend to employ inclusive language less than those who employ meaning-driven translation methods. An exception is the NRSV, a form-driven translation that takes a thoroughgoing approach to gender accuracy. Table 4.1 is a chart indicating how far various translations go in employing inclusive language.

POLITICAL CORRECTNESS

Two further concerns relating to political correctness are a desire to avoid unnecessary anti-Semitism and unnecessary prejudice against disabled people.

Jews or Jewish leaders? A sensitive issue is the translation of *ioudaioi*, frequently translated "Jews," found in the Gospels and Acts but

Table 4.1. Range of Inclusive Language in Various Translations

Nearly None	A Little	Partial	Thorough
AV/KJV			TEV (1992)
RSV	ESV		NRSV
NKJV	LB		NLT
JB		NJB	NAB
NEB		REB	*The Message*
Amplified		NET	ICB/NCV
NASB			CEV
NIV			NIVi/TNIV

most frequently in John's Gospel. Today's New International Version (see pp. 186-87) often renders this word by an alternative such as "Jewish leaders." A good example is found in John 9:22, where the parents of a blind man healed by Jesus are "afraid of the Jews" (NIV). The TNIV alters this to "afraid of the Jewish leaders." The reason for doing so is explained on the TNIV website:

> The TNIV translates the Greek *ioudaioi*—customarily rendered "the Jews"—with greater precision and sensitivity to context. Like many Greek words, *ioudaioi* has a range of meanings. Depending on the context, it can refer to one of the following:
> (1) Jewish people in general
> (2) A localized group of Jews
> (3) Jewish religious authorities
> In John 9:22, *ioudaioi* refers specifically to the Jewish religious authorities interrogating the blind man's parents, who were also Jewish (see 9:13-34). The TNIV's careful translation helps the reader understand the precise meaning of the text.[8]

The CEV translates *ioudaioi* in an even wider variety of ways: "leaders" (Jn 1:19-20; 18:36), "our people" (Jn 7:35), "in public" (for "openly among the Jews" in Jn 11:54), "everyone" (for "Jewish officials" in Jn 18:20) and "the crowd" (Jn 18:31). It is hard not to see in these choices a deliberate attempt to avoid a charge of anti-Semitism. While it is clear that in many or all of the instances cited, "the Jews" refers only to some

Jews or only to Jewish leaders, too great a concern for cultural sensitivities and political correctness can endanger accuracy of translation.[9]

Disabled people. Another concern has been raised by those who lobby for the physically disabled. It is now less acceptable to define a person according to their condition: a hemophiliac is a person with hemophilia, and an alcoholic, a person with alcohol dependency. Behind these changes in English usage there is an admirable desire to preserve the dignity of those afflicted and to recognize their full humanity.

Instead of "lepers," the NIV family of translations speaks of those who "have leprosy." As well as being more politically correct, this allows a footnote to be added to the effect that the Bible term *leprosy* refers to a large number of skin diseases, not just the disease known by that name today. The NRSV, ESV, NASB and NET retain the term *leper.* The NLT and CEV follow the NIV. The TEV and NCV speak of people with a "skin disease"; the HCSB of those with "a serious skin disease."

Certain other Bible terms present their own problems. To many, a paralytic is not a paralyzed person but someone who is roaring drunk. And someone who is dumb may not just be a person who has lost the power of speech but one who is lacking intelligence, at least in colloquial usage. More recent translations make changes as appropriate to avoid confusion and mirth.[10]

I have now covered the major issues involved in choosing a Bible translation. But before looking at the origins of the translations available to us, there are a few minor points to consider in the next chapter.

YET MORE CHOICES

The teachings of the Lord are perfect;

they give new strength.

The Lord's rules can be trusted;

they make plain people wise.

PSALM 19:7 NCV

In this chapter we will examine a few of the remaining issues to be faced when purchasing a Bible. These are of less importance than the issues covered thus far.

INDIVIDUAL OR COMMITTEE TRANSLATIONS?

Historically, most translations are either the product of a committee structure or the work of a single individual. All versions in the AV/KJV tradition are of the committee type. Paraphrases are always the work of an individual. Other translations fall into either category.

Naturally, committee translations draw on the expertise of a large number of scholars, usually several dozen, each crosschecking the work of others. Committee translations are less likely to show evidence of idiosyncratic renderings or sectarian bias. But committee translations can suffer from any of three problems. First, they are made by biblical exegetes rather than English-language specialists. Consultation with English stylists generally comes late in the process. Second, a committee structure has a leveling-out effect: the need for compromise between committee members tends toward a conservative approach and sometimes to a blandness of style. And third, in the case of revised versions, changes may be only cautiously accepted. Typically, revisions are accepted only if agreed on by a two-thirds majority of the translation committee.

In contrast, translations that are the work of an individual often have more vibrancy of style and make a greater impact. But they can be quirky and are open to the conscious or unconscious interpretive views of the translator. Some of the best translations are the work of an individual that has later been revised by a team of scholars. The AV/KJV itself, resting on the shoulders of William Tyndale, is the prime example. Another is the New Living Translation (see pp. 178-81).

EVANGELICAL, ECUMENICAL OR ROMAN CATHOLIC?

In some cases, committee translations are also thoroughly ecumenical, with scholars drawn from a wide theological and denominational spectrum. This is true of the RSV and its revision, the NRSV; and also of the NEB and its successor, the REB. In other cases (the NASB, NIV and ESV being evangelical examples) committee members are required to subscribe to a particular view of biblical inspiration. In the case of the JB, NJB and NAB, the majority of translators were Roman Catholics.

Ecumenical translations often have greater interdenominational support and participation than evangelical versions. The first translation to be officially accepted by both Protestant and Roman Catholic Churches was the Common Bible (an edition of the RSV with Apocrypha) in 1973. The further addition in 1977 of the books approved by the Eastern Orthodox Churches made it acceptable to them as well. Many evangelicals happily use the RSV and its successor, the NRSV.

Evangelical translations are those proposed and largely prepared by evangelical scholars. Some on the more conservative wing of the evangelical tradition go so far as to argue that only a translation prepared by those adhering to a high doctrine of the verbal inspiration of Scripture can be trusted.

Roman Catholic translations are those sponsored and largely translated by that denomination. The Roman Catholic Church awards an official *imprimatur* to translations it recommends for use by its congregations. More recent Catholic translations such as the JB have received widespread recognition outside that denomination.

Not all translations fit neatly into one of the above three categories. For instance, listed in appendix two are some Jewish translations of the Jewish Bible, to which Christians have given the name Old Testament. Another example is God's Word, a Lutheran-inspired version (see pp. 173-74).

THEOLOGICAL BIAS

Sometimes, concern is expressed over possible theological bias in particular translations. While there are a few sectarian translations (such as the New World Translation used by Jehovah's Witnesses; see pp. 149-50) that are clearly subject to bias, in general no reputable translator or translation committee would allow theological or denominational distortion into their work.

This, however, has not prevented accusations of bias from being made. William Tyndale, for instance, was accused of heresy for using *repent, love, elder*[1] and *congregation* instead of the church-approved phrasing *do penance, charity, priest* and *church* respectively. Today, in Paul's pastoral epistles, modern translations are still divided between *elder* versus *priest* and *overseer* versus *bishop.*

Concerns over theological or doctrinal bias run far deeper in North America than they do in Britain, no more so than over the Revised Standard Version (see pp. 142-47). Sadly, the split between those favoring an ecumenical translation and those favoring an evangelical one has never healed. To an extent, the present controversy over inclusive language has been fueled by a simplistic approach on the part of some conservatives to their understanding of the verbal inspiration of Scripture. How the unity of Scripture is understood also impinges on certain translation choices, as previously discussed on pages 85-88.

Far more than the wording of a verse here or there, how a translation is perceived is determined by the supplementary material appearing alongside the text. King James had good reason for insisting that the AV/ KJV be issued without margin notes: its rival, the Geneva Bible, was seen as pro-Reformed and anti-Catholic because of its notes. Both the evangelical NIV and the ecumenical NRSV come in study-Bible editions. It is the introductions and notes in these editions, rather than the biblical text itself, that give a translation a certain theological label, which then often determines who will or who won't use that particular version.

BOOKS OF THE APOCRYPHA

A further factor is the inclusion or omission of the books of the Apocrypha. Typically, evangelical translations omit the Apocrypha; ecumenical translations include them in just some editions (usually as a separate section between Old and New Testaments); and Roman Catholic Bibles always include them—or at least the writings deemed deuterocanonical[2]—interspersing them between other OT books.

The exact list of the writings accepted as authoritative varies across church traditions. The present *Catechism of the Roman Catholic Church* states that it "accepts and venerates as inspired the 46 books of the Old Testament."[3] By this is meant the thirty-nine books found in the Hebrew Bible plus seven further books, together with certain additions to Esther and Daniel: *Tobit, Judith, Wisdom of Solomon, Ecclesiasticus, Baruch, The Letter of Jeremiah* (= chap. 6 of *Baruch*), *First Maccabees* and *Second Maccabees*. The additions to Daniel are *The Prayer of Azariah and the Song of the Three Jews, Susanna* and *Bel and the Dragon*. There are six Greek additions to Esther that fit into various places within the usual Hebrew text: one before 1:1; one after 3:13; two after 4:17; one after 8:12; and one after 10:3. In addition, the Protestant Apocrypha includes *First and Second Esdras* and the *Prayer of Manasseh*.

These books and additions are not contained in the Hebrew Bible (the Christian Old Testament) but have come to us from the Septuagint (LXX), a Greek translation of the Old Testament dating from c. 250 to 100 B.C. The books of the Apocrypha also appear in the Latin Vulgate, a translation of the Bible prepared by Jerome in c. A.D. 380, and remained unchallenged as the basic text of the Bible until the Renaissance. The

books of the Apocrypha appeared as standard in all the major translations of the sixteenth and seventeenth centuries, including the AV/KJV.

Although Jesus and the writers of the New Testament quote exten-
sively from the Old Testament, they never quote directly from the
Apocrypha, though there are some allusions here and there. The Apocrypha was never accepted as being within the official list (or "canon")
of scriptural writings, either in Jewish or in early Christian tradition.
Referring to the Apocrypha, the sixth article of the Church of England
states, "And the other Books . . . the Church doth read for example of
life and instruction of manners; but yet doth it not apply them to es-
tablish any doctrine."

To make matters more complicated still, Bibles used by the Eastern
Orthodox Churches include yet further books and additions. One of
these is a psalm designated Psalm 151, which celebrates King David's
battle with Goliath. These can all be found in those editions of the
NRSV which contain the Apocrypha.

From an evangelical or Reformed viewpoint, a Bible with the Apocrypha cannot be recommended for regular use. The *Westminster Confession of Faith* (1647) says: "The books commonly called Apocrypha, not
being of divine inspiration, are no part of the Canon of Scripture; and
therefore are of no authority in the Church of God." Nevertheless, parts
of the Apocrypha are of interest, especially for understanding the four
hundred years of history between the Old and New Testaments. Table
5.1 shows where the Apocrypha is and is not included in Bible versions.

Table 5.1. The Inclusion or Omission of the Apocrypha in Various Bible Versions

In no editions	In some editions (between OT and NT)	In all editions (within the OT)
NIV/TNIV	AV/KJV	JB/NJB
NCV/ICB	RSV/NRSV	NAB
NASB	NEB/REB	CCB
The Message	LB/NLT	
GW	TEV	
	CEV	
	ESV (possibly future UK editions)	
	NET (in preparation)	

LOVE THY NEIGHBOUR

Most currently available translations originate in North America. Notable exceptions are the AV/KJV, the NEB/REB, the JB and NJB, and J. B. Phillips's New Testament paraphrase. Bible versions originating in America are generally anglicized for the U.K. market. Some Bibles, such as the CEV, are also available in special editions for Australia, New Zealand and other English-speaking countries.

When a Bible is anglicized, the most obvious change is to spelling. *Savior* becomes *Saviour, ax* becomes *axe* and *neighbor* turns into *neighbour*. Apart from running the text through a computer spell-checker, there are a few other differences between U.S. and U.K. English that should be noted. Table 5.2 shows some different vocabulary and expressions between British and American editions.

Table 5.2. British and American Variants in Translation

American	British
rooster	cock (NRSV)
gotten for gold	bought for gold (Job 28:15 NRSV)
to do their service	to perform their service (Num 8:22 NRSV)
earth on their heads	dust on their heads (Neh 9:1 NRSV)
grainfields	corn fields (Mt 12:1 NLT)
Jordan River	River Jordan (2 Kings 5:10, 12 NLT)
hucksters	hawkers (2 Cor 2:17 NLT)
in the six hundred first year	in the six hundred and first year (Gen 8:13 NRSV)

There are also a few changes to punctuation. American English often adds commas where British English omits them. Likewise, British English often employs hyphens where American English has two separate words.

Frankly, few British readers will have any problems with an American Bible, or vice versa. But it is nice to see words spelled the way you think they should be spelled! If you are concerned to have—or not to have—a particular edition, double-check before you buy.

STILL MORE CHOICES

As well as deciding which translation one wants, there are several other choices to be made when purchasing a Bible. A Bible can be a brilliant translation, but if the text is not thoughtfully presented, a reader will quickly look for another from the bookshop shelf.

Presentation. Externally, color and cover design are largely a matter of personal taste. Durability is perhaps more important. Bibles come in paperback, hardback and various qualities of leather. Paperback Bibles are rarely a good investment. Treat either a hardback or a leather Bible well and it will last for many years. Because leather absorbs the oils from your skin, leather-bound Bibles last longer the more they are handled. (There is a sermon illustration here somewhere!) The more popular translations are available in a range of sizes, from pocket to pulpit editions. While a pocket Bible is smaller and lighter to carry, the print size might be too small.

Internally, a vital consideration is readability. Can the print be read in poor light and without strain? Special large-print Bibles are available in a number of translations for the visually impaired. And for those with very poor sight, an audio Bible is an option to consider. But even for those with good eyesight, a clear and attractive page layout is a considerable blessing in any Bible.

Columns and margins. In some Bibles, instead of the traditional double-column arrangement, a single-column layout is preferred. The NEB is one example. Generally, however, a narrower newspaper-style double column makes it easier for the eye to scan a section of text to locate a particular word, phrase or verse number. It also makes reading aloud easier. Some Bibles have extra-wide margins to accommodate note taking, but some ink may bleed through particularly thin paper.

Red letter. A red-letter Bible has the words of Christ printed in red. This practice goes back to 1899, when Louis Klopsch prepared a red-letter AV/KJV New Testament for publication in New York. There is, however, little justification for this custom: the whole Bible is God's Word.

Naturally, in red-letter Bibles there is a concentration of red ink in the Gospels. Bruce Metzger rightly comments: "Such a procedure not only destroys the unity of the text . . . but also implies a theological judgement that what Jesus said is more significant than what he did."[4]

Section headings. Until the 1970s, most Bibles presented the text as a solid block. Since then, most Bible printers have used a variety of devices to break up the text. Apart from illustrations (such as the TEV's famous line-drawings), the most common device is the section heading, also called a crossheading.

Most Bibles, in their introduction, rightly draw attention to the fact that such headings do not form a part of the scriptural text and should not be read aloud in church use. While they break up what would otherwise be an unrelieved wall of print, they can impose a form and shape to the text that is not always helpful. Reference has been made already to the section heading that appears in several Bibles just before Romans 1:18, despite the Greek indicating continuity with the previous verses (see p. 52). The TNIV has moved several section headings that had been deemed misplaced in the NIV.

Section headings can improve the visual appearance of a page and help a reader locate a particular passage, but they also need to be treated with some skepticism. The best advice is to think of them as being invisible. They are certainly not infallible.[5]

Cross-references and concordances. Cross-references are a valuable tool in any Bible. They take the reader from one passage to others with similar key words, phrases or ideas. Reading the introduction will explain how the cross-reference system is best used.

Similar to cross-references, but working in a slightly different way, are chain references and thematic references. These allow the user to trace a particular topic or theme through Scripture. Best-known is the *Thompson Chain Reference Bible.* Much better, however, in my opinion, is the *NIV Thematic Study Bible*,[6] available either in print form or on CD-ROM.

A built-in concordance, however brief, can also be useful in locating half-remembered verses or undertaking word studies. More comprehensive, stand-alone concordances are of even greater value.

Study Bibles. A study Bible is certainly worth considering when buying a new Bible. Most include cross-references and many have a concordance, but they will also have book introductions, outlines and study notes giving historical background and commentary on the text. Take advice from your minister or Christian bookshop about which might best suit you. Every study Bible, however, has a particular theological slant and can limit the way we look at God's Word.[7] Have at least one copy of your favorite translation in an edition *without* any study notes; it is sometimes a good idea to learn to rely more on the Spirit and a little less on scholarly dissection.

Electronic Bibles. My smallest Bible is a little under 2 millimeters thick. It is not that the paper is incredibly thin; in fact, this Bible is not made of paper at all. It is entirely on CD-ROM. Almost every Bible translation discussed in this book is available in an electronic format as well as in traditional printed form. Indeed, there are some versions that are only (or primarily) available in electronic editions. Some are discussed on pages 194-97. The most notable is the NET Bible.

Translations can be viewed or downloaded from the Internet. Many have dedicated websites (see pp. 224-25). Sample passages can usually be inspected, helping you decide before buying the full print version. Complete electronic Bibles can also be purchased on CD-ROM for use on desktop, laptop and even handheld computers. Such Bibles typically come with powerful search and study tools. A useful feature is the ability to drop Bible verses into other documents. Resources are listed in appendix three. All in all, there is no reason not to have a Bible, either printed or electronic, immediately available at one's fingertips!

And the range of choice does not end there. It is not quite limitless, and there are some restrictions: you cannot, for example, buy an REB with cross-references or an NJB without the Apocrypha—such editions do not exist. But with other Bibles the range of editions available is almost overwhelming. Here is a full checklist of questions to consider.

- Do I want a complete Bible, just the New Testament, or the New Testament with the Psalms?
- Do I want a Bible with or without the Apocrypha?
- Is a plain text Bible what I want, or a full study Bible, or one with devotional notes?

- What about a concordance, cross-references or both?
- Do I want maps?
- Do I want wide margins for notetaking?
- Do I want the words of Christ in red?
- What binding do I want: paperback, hardback or leather?
- What size of Bible do I want: standard, pocket or large print?
- Could I use an electronic Bible for my desktop or handheld computer?

One further issue is that of the underlying Hebrew or Greek text. It will be discussed in more detail in appendix one but will close this chapter.

WHICH ORIGINALS?

Open almost any Bible and there will be a number of footnotes across the bottom of the page. There are two principal reasons for this: (1) there is a genuine difference of opinion over how the Hebrew or Greek should be translated; or (2) there is uncertainty as to what the original Hebrew or Greek might actually have been.

The question of how translators sift through the textual evidence available to them in countless Hebrew, Greek and other manuscripts will be left to appendix one. However, some comments are in order here.

First, many documents have come to light since 1611, one of the most significant discoveries being the Dead Sea Scrolls in 1947. Older translations, notably the AV/KJV, may not always rest on the best available manuscript evidence. This alone provides a good reason for choosing a modern translation. The best modern versions of the New Testament use the most up-to-date editions of the Greek text, but a few modern versions opt for the same text that underlies the AV/KJV, thus perpetuating the problem of the AV/KJV's inaccuracy. The chief culprit here is the NKJV (see pp. 162-63). Some Old Testament versions stick very close to the Hebrew "Masoretic" text, while others are happy to follow alternatives offered by the ancient translations (such as the Greek Septuagint) and conjectural emendations put forward by textual scholars when the Hebrew appears to have become corrupted or makes little sense.

One or two other translations have made some rather quirky textual choices. The NEB is a case in point (see the discussion on page 147-49). To summarize, nearly all modern translations are made from the best available Hebrew and Greek manuscript evidence, thus ensuring their accuracy. Beware of the one or two that do not follow this practice. See the end of appendix one for a discussion of passages, such as the ending of Mark's Gospel, which appears in some translations but are relegated to the footnotes in others.

PART TWO
Translations in English

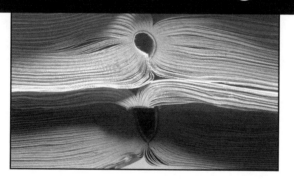

FROM UNAUTHORIZED
TO AUTHORIZED

Search the Scriptures, for in them ye think ye have eternal life:
and they are they which testify of me.

JOHN 5:39, TRANSLATED BY WILLIAM TYNDALE, 1534

This second part of the book gets down to the business of looking at actual Bible translations. This will be more or less in historical order, but with only a brief look at the earliest English versions of the Bible in order to concentrate on those that are available today. This chapter considers the translations leading up to the Authorized (King James) Version of 1611.

OLD ENGLISH VERSIONS

In his *Ecclesiastical History of the English People,* the Venerable Bede (672-735) tells of Caedmon, a laborer attached to the abbey of Whitby in Yorkshire. In a dream, God granted Caedmon gifts of poetry and song. In acknowledgment of this gift, he was made a full monk of the abbey. Thereafter, according to Bede, whenever Caedmon was taught "a passage of scriptural history or doctrine" he would "render it into verse if he could."[1]

It seems that what Caedmon sang were metrical paraphrases of Scripture passages and themes. These were translated not from Hebrew or Greek but from the Latin used by the church at that time and up to the Reformation. The tongue in which Caedmon sang was Anglo-Saxon (or Old English), a language far removed from the English spoken today. Other poets produced similar paraphrases from Caedmon's time through to the tenth century. Only a late ninth-century West Saxon[2] version of one of Caedmon's hymns has survived to the present; otherwise the content of his verse is unknown.

Bede himself is credited with producing a written translation of John's Gospel. According to Cuthbert, Bishop of Lindisfarne, Bede completed this work on the day he died in 735.[3] Bede is thought to have translated other Bible portions, including perhaps the Lord's Prayer, for the benefit of monks whose Latin was poor. None survives. Aldhelm (640-709), a contemporary of Bede and the first Bishop of Sherborne, Dorset, is credited with a translation of the Psalms (c. 700-705). Alfred the Great (king from 871 to 901) published a law code introduced by his own translation of the Ten Commandments. It also includes other extracts from Exodus and a few verses from Acts. He is also said to have translated some of the Psalms toward the end of his life.

There is, in the British Library, a priceless eighth-century copy of the Psalms in Latin: the Vespasian Psalter, which I have had the privilege of holding in my hands. At some later date, probably in the ninth century, an English translation was added between the lines, a form of translation termed *interlinear gloss*. A similar word-for-word translation appears in the magnificently illuminated Lindisfarne Gospels, also housed in the British Library. These were copied from the Latin Vulgate c. A.D. 715 and were the work of Eadfrith, Cuthbert's successor as Bishop of Lindisfarne. At some point in the mid-tenth century, a priest named Aldred inserted a literal English rendering between the Latin lines. A similar gloss—in fact an exact copy of the Lindisfarne gloss in three out of the four Gospels—appears in the Rushworth Gospels, now kept in Oxford's Bodleian Library.

From the same period comes the first independent Old English version of the Gospels, known as the Wessex Gospels. William Tyndale (see pp. 118-21) believed these to have been made at the command of Alfred's grandson, Athelstan, arguably the first king of a truly united England. A few decades later, toward the end of the tenth century, Abbot Aelfric of Eynsham in Oxfordshire translated the first seven books of the Bible, Genesis to Judges.

JOHN WYCLIFFE

Following the Norman invasion of England in 1066, the English language changed considerably. The ruling classes spoke Norman French, deeply influencing the English spoken by the rest of the population. Old English gave way to Middle English. Few translations of any part of the Bible were made. Those that were made were very elaborate and lengthy poetic paraphrases set alongside romanticized stories of famous lives. Apart from two translations of the Psalms—one metrical and one in prose—the most significant translations of this period are the ones associated with John Wycliffe (c. 1324-1384).

Wycliffe (also spelled Wyclif) has been dubbed the "Morning Star of the Reformation." A distinguished Oxford academic, he became rector of Lutterworth, Leicestershire, and gained widespread support for his outspoken criticism of the papacy, which by then was growing increasingly corrupt.

Wycliffe argued that the laws of the Bible were more important than the laws of the church. He began to write in English instead of Latin and organized a group of itinerant preachers, or "poor priests," who spread his ideas through the country. His supporters were later mockingly called Lollards, from the Dutch meaning "mumblers."

Two Bible versions are linked to Wycliffe, though how much of either is his direct work is hard to know. Copies of the first appeared between 1380 and 1384. Much of the Old Testament is known to be the work of Nicholas of Hereford, a Wycliffe supporter; it is conceivable that other parts of the Old Testament and some of the New Testament might be the work of Wycliffe himself. Even if not, however, it is clear that it was his zeal for making the Scriptures accessible that gave impetus to the work.

Although a very literal translation, with relatively poor and uneven English and a Latin accent, it does have the distinction of being the first complete Bible in any form of the English language. It is, however, a translation from the Latin Vulgate, not from the Hebrew and Greek. And since the work was completed nearly a century before the invention of printing, every copy put into circulation—of which there were many—was laboriously handwritten.

The translation was gradually revised, reaching its final form in 1388, four years after Wycliffe's death. Some believe this to be the work of John Purvey, another of his followers, but there is no hard evidence for this. David Daniell suggests that John Trevisa, another Oxford scholar, is a more likely candidate.[4] This was a much smoother translation and proved very popular. It was not superseded until Tyndale translated the New Testament 150 years later.

A failed attempt to put Wycliffe on trial was made in 1378. A second attempt in 1382 was more successful. Some of Wycliffe's supporters had not sufficiently distanced themselves from the peasant revolts led by Wat Tyler the previous year, in which the Archbishop of Canterbury had been killed. In a church convocation, Wycliffe was pronounced a heretic, forcing him to retreat to his Lutterworth rectory, where he remained until his death.

During his latter years, he continued to write prolifically. These writings were later condemned by a Church Council in 1414, which ordered Wycliffe's bones to be dug up, burned and thrown into the River Swift. Copies of his Bible were also frequently burned, but judging by the number of manuscripts that have survived, the translation was clearly widely circulated and widely read.

WILLIAM TYNDALE

No one has made more impact on the translation of the Bible into English than William Tyndale (c. 1494-1536), who paid for his effort with his life. In following the history of English Bible translation from Tyndale to the AV/KJV, it is worth holding in mind the dates and religious leanings of the relevant monarchs (see table 6.1).

Table 6.1. English Monarchs from Tyndale to the AV/KJV

Monarch	Reign	Religious leaning	Major historical significance
Henry VIII	1509-1547	Catholic at first	Broke with Rome in 1534
Edward VI	1547-1553	Fervent Protestant	—
Mary I	1553-1558	Fervent Catholic	Known as "Bloody Mary"
Elizabeth I	1558-1603	Protestant	—
James I	1603-1625	Protestant	= James VI of Scotland

Born in Gloucestershire, Tyndale was educated at Oxford, gaining his master's degree in 1515. This was a time of ferment across Europe. Humanism had led to a Renaissance in culture and learning. As well as celebrating the arts and sciences, there was an eager desire to re-examine the original sources of human knowledge, all considerably helped by the introduction of printing in the late fifteenth century.[5] This called for the learning of languages such as Greek and Hebrew alongside the well-established Latin. Erasmus (1466-1536), one of the greatest humanist scholars, produced the first printed Greek New Testament in 1515.

In 1517, Martin Luther nailed his famous ninety-five theses to the door of the castle church in Wittenberg, Germany. This was the spark that ignited the Protestant Reformation, leading eventually to the English Church's break with Rome. In his theses, Luther attacked the Catholic practice of selling indulgences, believed to secure the forgiveness of sins and a reduction in the time a soul spent in purgatory. Through studying the Bible, Luther had come to believe in salvation through grace alone and justification by faith alone.

Luther translated the New Testament into German—not the German used in courtly circles but the vernacular German used by ordinary, working people. Luther's translation first appeared in print in 1522 and gained instant popularity. It is often called the September Testament after the month in which it was published.

Tyndale set his mind to do the same in English, aiming to produce first a printed New Testament in everyday language and then, if possible, a complete Bible. In a debate with an unnamed opponent, Tyndale was told that "we were better be without God's Law than the Pope's." Tyndale retorted, "I defy the Pope and all his laws. If God spare my life, before many years I will make sure that a boy who drives the plough knows more of the Scriptures than you do."[6]

In 1523 Tyndale approached the Bishop of London, Cuthbert Tunstall, for support in translating the Bible into English. The bishop refused, and Tyndale went to continental Europe to undertake his work. The printing of his New Testament began in 1524 in Cologne, Germany, but opposition forced him to flee to the city of Worms with the unbound sheets.

At least three thousand complete New Testaments were printed in Worms between 1525 and 1526. These were smuggled into England in bales of cloth, carried down the Rhine and across the Channel to English ports. Some were found and seized. In November 1526 Bishop Tunstall preached at a ceremony in St. Paul's during which copies were publicly burned. Many copies that did reach eager hands were read until they fell apart.[7]

After Worms, Tyndale next moved to the safety of Antwerp. Having now learned Hebrew as well as Greek, he published his translation of the books of Moses (Genesis to Deuteronomy) in 1530; the book of Jonah followed in 1531; and the Old Testament historical books (Joshua to 2 Chronicles) were completed by 1535. These, however, were not printed until after his death.

In 1534 Tyndale produced a carefully revised and much improved edition of his New Testament. (A modern-spelling edition of this has been prepared by David Daniell.[8]) Together with Tyndale's work on the Old Testament, this New Testament formed the basis of many subsequent translations, including all those leading up to the King James Version and its more recent revisions. Bruce Metzger describes Tyndale's translation as "free, bold and idiomatic."[9] It is certainly not as word-for-word as some imagine it to be.

In 1535 Henry (or Harry) Phillips tricked Tyndale into arrest. A recent biographer of Tyndale, Brian Moynahan, believes Henry VIII's Chancellor Thomas More to have been behind Phillips's treachery.[10] Tyndale was imprisoned near Brussels for some eighteen months. He was executed on October 6, 1536. Foxe's *Book of Martyrs* gives this account: "He was brought forth to the place of execution, was there tied to the stake, and then strangled first by the hangman, and afterwards with fire consumed, crying thus at the stake with a fervent zeal and a loud voice, 'Lord, open the King of England's eyes.'"

What Tyndale could not have known was that an answer to his prayer was already unfolding. Earlier that year Henry VIII had given permission for the distribution of the first complete printed English Bible, one which drew in large measure from Tyndale's own efforts.

THE COVERDALE BIBLE (1535)

The first full Bible in English was produced in 1535 by Miles Coverdale (1488-1569). Henry VIII had broken all ties with the Pope. Thomas More, who had opposed Henry's marriage to Anne Boleyn, had been executed on a charge of treason. Anne, influenced by Henry's new Chancellor and parliamentarian Thomas Cromwell, favored an English Bible.

In December 1534 the new Archbishop of Canterbury, Thomas Cranmer, together with other clergy had petitioned the king for a translation of the Bible in English. They did not care much for Tyndale's translation, but they did see the need for an officially sanctioned Bible. Coverdale's Bible, printed in Europe, at least temporarily fitted the bill. A dedication to Henry was inserted in imported copies.

Coverdale was nowhere near the scholar Tyndale had been. Coverdale made no pretense at knowing any Hebrew or Greek and worked from the Latin in consultation with Luther's and other German translations. Tyndale's influence is clearly evident in the New Testament and the books of Moses. Notable features of Coverdale's Bible are the introduction of chapter-by-chapter summaries and the inclusion of the Apocrypha in a separate section between the Old and New Testaments. The final books of the New Testament follow the same arrangement as in Tyndale and Luther: Hebrews, James, Jude and Revelation are placed in a semi-separate section after the letters of Peter and John, reflecting Luther's skepticism about their value as Scripture. Coverdale's version of the Psalms has come down to us via the Great Bible (1539) into the 1662 *Book of Common Prayer*. It was Coverdale who gave us "the valley of the shadowe of death" and "enoyntest my heade with oyle" in Psalm 23:4-5.

Coverdale's translation did not remain popular for long. Anne Boleyn, its major supporter, was beheaded in May 1536. Further printings did, however, appear in 1537, 1550 and 1553.

MATTHEW'S BIBLE (1537)

Cranmer urged that a royal license be granted to a new Bible which appeared in 1537 and would again temporarily fill the need for an English Bible that Cranmer hoped to produce. The new Bible was attributed to Thomas Matthew, a pen name for a former associate of Tyndale named John Rogers. Matthew's Bible contains even more of Tyndale's work than Coverdale's; as well as including Tyndale's New Testament and books of Moses, it also printed for the first time the historical books of the Old Testament that Tyndale had translated but not published before his martyrdom. The full-page initials W. T., which appear at the end of the Old Testament, are a tribute to Tyndale. The rest of the work is largely Coverdale's, Rogers being little more than an editor.

The royal license covered not only Matthew's Bible but also the 1537 edition of Coverdale. John Rogers himself was later burned at the stake in 1555, the first of many Protestant martyrs in the reign of the Catholic "Bloody" Queen Mary.

TAVERNER'S BIBLE (1539)

A further revision of Matthew's Bible was issued by Richard Taverner in 1539. Taverner (c. 1505-1575) enjoyed the support of Thomas Cromwell. He was a good Greek scholar, and his New Testament was an improvement on Matthew's. In fact, Daniell argues that Taverner's Bible should be regarded as a more or less original version in its own right, not merely an updating of Matthew's Bible.[11] Certainly, Taverner's version of the Apocrypha differs considerably from that of Coverdale or Matthew. One phrase of Taverner's Bible that has survived into the AV/KJV is found in Hebrews 1:3, where Jesus is called the "express image" of God. He also changed Tyndale's "similitude" into "parable."

Taverner's Bible was the first to be actually printed on English soil. But Coverdale's, Matthew's and Taverner's Bibles were all to be eclipsed by the Great Bible, which appeared just a few months after Taverner's work.

THE GREAT BIBLE (1539)

In 1538 Henry issued a decree that a Bible "of the greatest volume" be set up in every parish church. A revision of Matthew's Bible, but without its outspoken Protestant notes, was prepared for this purpose. Thus, ironically, the work of William Tyndale became available in every church in the land just three years after his death.

The task of editing the Great Bible was entrusted to Coverdale on the invitation of Thomas Cromwell. It and all others since have the books of the New Testament in the order familiar today instead of Luther's arrangement. It is sometimes called the Whitchurch Bible after the name of its printer.

So popular was the Great Bible that people gathered around it to hear it being read, and to hold impromptu public Bible studies, even if this entailed interrupting a church service to do so! The second, improved edition of 1540, and subsequent editions, have a preface written by Archbishop Cranmer. The Psalms of the Great Bible have been perpetuated in the Anglican *Book of Common Prayer.*

BISHOP BECKE'S BIBLE (1551)

A version known as Bishop Becke's Bible appeared in 1551, dedicated to Edward VI. Essentially Tyndale's New Testament combined with the Old Testament of Taverner's Bible, its only new feature was interpretive marginal notes. It is also known as the "Wife-Beater's Charter" on account of an unhappy interpretation of 1 Peter 3:7 in which men are exhorted to live with their wives "according to knowledge." According to Becke's notes, if a wife is not helpful and obedient to her husband, he should endeavor "to beate the feare of God into her heade."

THE GENEVA BIBLE (1560)

With the coronation of the fervently Catholic Mary in 1553, English Protestants fled to Geneva, Switzerland, the center of Reformed Protestantism. The Geneva New Testament appeared in 1557, and a complete Bible with revised New Testament followed in 1560. The New Testament is generally credited to the oversight of William Whittingham, brother-in-law to the great Reformation theologian John Calvin. The Geneva Bible is also known as the Breeches Bible in view of its translation of Genesis 3:7: "They sewed figge-tree leaves together and made themselves breeches."

The Geneva Bible was the first to have numbered verses. And because it did, it was able to offer valuable cross-references. It also employed Roman type instead of the more usual black-letter (or Gothic) typeface, which made it much easier to read. Another feature, which would be continued in the AV/KJV, was the printing in italic of words not found in the Hebrew or Greek but supplied to make sense in English. It was also the first English Bible to be translated wholly from the Hebrew and Greek. (Coverdale's and Matthew's Bible, along with the Great Bible, depended on the Latin for the translation of Old Testament books after 2 Chronicles.)

Most notable, however, was the inclusion of a large number of marginal annotations, making it a favored Protestant study Bible. A few of these notes—though not as many as is sometimes suggested—had an antipapal bias. Because of these features and its low cost, the Geneva Bible met with immediate success and popularity. Large numbers were imported into England; it was also the first Bible to be printed in Scotland (in 1579), where there was Protestant support.

From its publication in 1560, the Geneva Bible reigned supreme in Protestant affections for over a century. New editions appeared almost yearly. A revised New Testament appeared in 1576. Even after the publication of the AV/KJV in 1611, the Geneva Bible remained the favored choice of many Protestants and Puritans. Editions from 1599 contained a very full commentary on the book of Revelation, selected quotations from which have given it its undeserved anti-Catholic reputation.

The Geneva Bible was the Bible used by Shakespeare, Spenser, Milton and Bunyan, and was the one taken by the Pilgrim Fathers in the *Mayflower* when they set sail from Plymouth, England, to America in 1620.

THE BISHOPS' BIBLE (1568)

Irked by the popularity of the Geneva Bible, Matthew Parker, archbishop of Canterbury, initiated a revision of the Great Bible. Production took four years, from 1564 to 1568. Like the Great Bible before it, large and impressive copies were placed in English parish churches. The quality of translation was uneven, however, due mostly to the lack of supervision given to the revisers. Some adhered closely to the Great Bible; others departed from it in an overly free way. The New Testament is generally better than the Old Testament. Parker was a Latin scholar, not an English stylist, and this shows in the wordiness and overall blandness of his translation. Gerald Hammond is damning in his review: "For the most part the Bishops' Bible is either a lazy and ill-informed collation of what had gone before, or, in its original parts, the work of a third-rate scholar and second-rate writers."[12]

Anglican worshipers were by now used to reciting the Psalms according to the wording of the Great Bible (adopted for the *Book of Common Prayer*, first published under Edward VI in 1549 and revived under Elizabeth I). In 1572, a somewhat improved edition of the Bishops' Bible appeared, with a revised New Testament and the Psalms of the Great Bible printed in parallel to its own. Most later editions included only the Psalms of the Great Bible.

After the Great Bible, the Bishops' Bible was the second "authorized" version, with the wording "Appointed to be read in the churches" on its title page.[13] The stage was set for a third that would dominate the religious landscape well into the twentieth century. Before that, however, we must note the appearance of the first Catholic Bible in the English language.

THE DOUAI-RHEIMS BIBLE (1610)

While persecution under Mary sent Protestants into exile at Geneva, persecution under Elizabeth sent Catholics into exile in Flanders (an area in and around modern Belgium). A training center for English priests was established at Douai, where Catholic scholars made a translation of the Bible. In 1578 the college moved to Rheims, where the translation was completed in 1582 under the leadership of Jesuit academic Gregory Martin. Because of a lack of money, only the New Testament was printed; the complete Bible did not appear until 1610, by which time the college had moved back to Douai.

Like all Catholic Bibles until the Jerusalem Bible of 1966, the Douai (or Douai-Rheims) Bible was prepared from the Latin Vulgate. It contains many barely translated Latin words and expressions, such as *pasch* for Passover (Acts 12:3) and *supersubstantial* for daily bread (Mt 6:11). One word that survived into the AV/KJV is *Paraclete,* Jesus' title for the Holy Spirit in John's Gospel. However, large parts of the Douai-Rheims New Testament are at least as dependent on Tyndale as they are on the Latin.

Further revisions of the Douai-Rheims Bible appeared over the years that followed, the most far-reaching being a revision undertaken by Bishop Richard Challoner in the middle of the eighteenth century (see p. 133).

THE KING JAMES BIBLE (1611)

In 1603 James VI of Scotland took over the English throne from the Tudors and was crowned James I of England, the first Stuart king. At the time, the number of English translations available was a source of religious disunity. By now the division of the church was not so much between Catholic and Protestant but between Protestant and Puritan. The Puritans wanted even deeper reforms of the English church, particularly in its liturgy and hierarchical structures. They later opposed the so-called divine right of kings.

It was in the interest of both the bishops and the Puritans to press the new king for a fresh translation, one which it was hoped would replace both the Geneva version and the Bishops' Bible, and also see off the Catholic challenge symbolized by the Douai-Rheims Bible. This they did at a conference convened by James at Hampton Court in January 1604. James agreed, and it was proposed that the Bishop's Bible be revised and "as little altered as the truth of the original will allow." While the translations of Tyndale, Matthew, Coverdale and the Great Bible were to be consulted, it was stipulated that there should be no interpretive marginal notes, only necessary explanations of the Hebrew and Greek.

The work was entrusted to six panels of scholars, two meeting at Oxford, two at Cambridge and two at Westminster. Of these panels, two looked after the New Testament, three the Old Testament and one the Apocrypha. Around fifty scholars in all were involved. When each panel finished its work, it was sent to all the rest for comment and revision. Final decisions were made by a general meeting of the chief members of all six panels. This method of translation set an important precedent for subsequent Bible versions, many of which have followed a similar committee approach to crosschecking and final editing.

Although approved in 1604, the work did not actually get into gear until 1607. Perhaps they were spurred into action by the religious ferment of 1605, including the Gunpowder Plot, a conspiracy to blow up the English Parliament and King James I on November 5, 1605, the day set for the king to open Parliament. The translation was, after that, completed in a little under three years, a truly remarkable achievement.

The lengthy preface to the AV/KJV (worth reading in full though it appears infrequently in modern editions) states clearly that it was not the aim to make "a new translation, nor yet to make of a bad one a good one . . . but to make a good one better, or out of many good ones one principal good one." Although a composite revision of preceding Bibles (and nominally a revision of the Bishops' Bible), it is the work of Tyndale that dominates the AV/KJV. An analysis made in 1998 demonstrates that Tyndale's words account for 84 percent of the New Testament and 75 percent of those Old Testament books that he translated.[14] His genius as a translator shines through in page after page and phrase after phrase. Many of his phrases have become proverbial and are in common use even by those who have little idea of their biblical origin (see p. 45).

Bruce Metzger says of the AV/KJV that a great deal of the praise belongs to its predecessors: "For the idiom and vocabulary, Tyndale deserves the greatest credit; for the melody and harmony, Coverdale; for scholarship and accuracy, the Geneva version."[15] The AV/KJV is at its best when it stays closest to Tyndale. It is weakest when it does not: portions of those parts of the Old Testament that Tyndale did not translate, particularly in the prophetic books, are close to unintelligible. The relationship between the Bibles preceding the AV/KJV are summarized in figure 6.1.

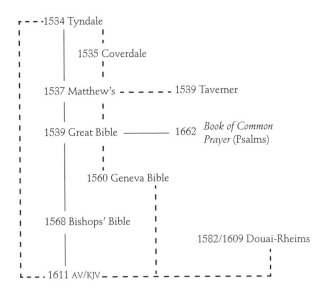

Figure 6.1. English Bibles leading up to the Authorized (King James) Version

Today, the AV/KJV is admired for its great literary English. The truth, however, is that it was written in everyday language to be understood by the common people. Most who came to love the AV/KJV did so through hearing it, not reading it; it must be remembered that only a small minority—perhaps fewer than one in four out of an English-speaking population of no more than six million—could read or write for themselves. But precisely because it was a version designed to be read aloud, it employed punchy, pithy language that is still rhythmic and memorable.

It would be wrong, however, to think that the AV/KJV was written in the language of its own day. Dependent on earlier translations, its language was already dated by the time of publication. For instance, *thou* and *ye* were already falling into disuse by 1611, as was the third-person singular verbal ending *-eth*. Its language is Elizabethan, not Jacobean.

Many assume the AV/KJV to be a very literal translation. While it is certainly more literal than some, it is not slavishly literal and in places is quite idiomatic.[16] To only a slightly lesser degree than Tyndale himself, his revisers deliberately employed a variety of English words when translating one Hebrew or Greek word. Likewise, they use the same English word for different words in the original.

The AV/KJV avoids the Latinisms favored by those of a Catholic persuasion and found in the Douai-Rheims Bible and to a lesser extent in the Bishops' Bible. For the same political reasons, it also avoids the nonconformist preferences of the Puritans, such as "washing" for "baptism," "congregation" for "church," "elder" for "priest" and "love" for "charity." It did, however, follow Tyndale and keep "repent" for "do penance" (see p. 103).

The AV/KJV begins each verse on a new line. Paragraphs are marked only by a special sign—¶—called a pilcrow. Oddly, these disappear after Acts 20:36. (Perhaps the printer ran out of them!)

A number of misprints found their way into some editions. Reference has already been made to the "He" and "She" editions, brought about by a variant reading in Ruth 3:15 (see p. 90). But the most infamous misprint is found in the so-called Wicked Bible of 1631, for which its printers were fined a then-enormous sum of three hundred pounds for omitting the word *not* from the seventh of the Ten Commandments, making it read, "Thou shalt commit adultery." Another misprint that has never been corrected is found in Matthew 23:24, which still reads "strain *at* a gnat" instead of "strain *out* a gnat."

For some, the AV/KJV is the only Bible. But while it will forever hold a preeminent place in the history of the English Bible, and despite its rich cadences that still retain their exquisite beauty, readers should remember four things, already mentioned in part one of this book:

- It is based on a defective text, especially in the Greek of the New Testament.
- Our understanding of Hebrew and Greek has grown significantly in the past four centuries.
- The English language has changed considerably over the same period of time.
- It was not the first English translation, or an original one, but a revision of several previous versions.

The first, the technical question of the original text underlying particular translations, will be further discussed in appendix one. But the second and third points can be illustrated here.

In 1 Samuel 13:21 the AV/KJV translates the rare Hebrew word *pîm* as "file," yielding the translation, "They had a *file* for the mattocks, and for the coulters [plough blades], and for the forks, and for the axes, and to sharpen the goads." More recent archaeology has revealed that a *pîm* was a metal weight used for business transactions in ancient Palestine. Worth two-thirds of a shekel (and weighing about a quarter of an ounce or 7.5 grams), it was the amount charged by a blacksmith for sharpening the agricultural implements listed.

It is hardly necessary to say how the word "gay" has changed in the English language since 1611. James 2:2, part of an injunction against favoritism, is rendered in the AV/KJV as "And ye have respect to him that weareth the gay clothing, and say unto him, Sit thou here in a good place." Most modern versions offer "fine clothing" as a more suitable contemporary translation. Another phrasing bound to raise an eyebrow if read aloud is the AV/KJV's translation of 1 Samuel 18:4: "Jonathan stripped . . . to his girdle" ("girdle" = "belt"). And for those who are still not convinced, try reading the AV/KJV's translation of 1 Samuel 25:22, 34 out loud in church one Sunday. In these verses men and boys are collectively defined as "any that pisseth against the wall"!

Notwithstanding these comments, the AV/KJV has served the church and the English-speaking public well for almost four centuries. Today's versions are often being revised within twenty years or less. As we progress with the history of English translations, we will see just how valuable and strong a legacy Tyndale and his revisers have left to subsequent versions.

7

CROSSING THE CENTURIES

Understand this, at the outset, that no prophetic scripture allows a man to
interpret it by himself; for prophecy never came by human impulse, it was
when carried away by the holy Spirit that the holy men of God spoke.

2 Peter 2:20-21, Moffatt

The publication of the AV/KJV is followed by a relatively quiet period
in terms of Bible translation. It is not until the mid-twentieth century
that things heat up again. Having become more popular than the
Geneva Bible by the mid-seventeenth century, the AV/KJV reigned supreme for over three hundred years. Indeed, it was not until as recently
as 1988 that it lost its place as the world's bestselling Bible. (Chapter
nine will reveal which translation eventually succeeded in knocking
the AV/KJV off the top spot.)

However, these centuries were not utterly silent, as far as Bible
translation goes. This chapter will cover the main developments up to
and including the 1952 Revised Standard Version. Many developments
during this period had more to do with incorporating the latest Greek
manuscript discoveries than with altering the style of the AV/KJV, a
style which became deeply embedded in the English mind and in
church liturgical practice.

Revisions of the av/kjv
In light of new textual discoveries, revisions of the AV/KJV were pub-

lished by several eighteenth-century scholars: Daniel Whitby (1703); Edward Wells (1718-1724); Daniel Mace (1729); and William Whiston (1745), Sir Isaac Newton's successor in the chair of mathematics at Cambridge, who titled his work the *Primitive New Testament*.

In 1768, John Wesley issued a revised edition of the AV/KJV, containing some twelve thousand alterations. It divided the biblical text into paragraphs and had notes for "plain, unlettered men who understand only their mother tongue." In 1840, Unitarian scholar Samuel Sharpe produced his own revision of the AV/KJV New Testament. His revision of the Old Testament followed in 1865.

Nor should we imagine that the AV/KJV itself remained unchanged. Revisions were made in 1613, 1629, 1638 and 1653. In 1701 dates were introduced into the margin based on the calculations of Bishop Ussher, including the dating of creation as 4004 B.C. Later corrections were made mostly as the result of changing English spelling and punctuation, including a far-reaching revision in 1762 by Thomas Price and Benjamin Blayney, among others. Blayney's AV/KJV is still the standard edition.

DOUAI-RHEIMS-CHALLONER

An English translation of the Bible for Roman Catholics completed in 1610 (see p. 126) received a major overhaul when a thoroughgoing revision was prepared by Bishop Richard Challoner, Vicar Apostolic of the London District. Challoner published five successive editions of the New Testament between 1749 and 1772, and two of the Old Testament, in 1750 and 1763. His revision shows evidence of having been influenced by the AV/KJV, but many of the Latin expressions of the earlier edition remain. It is a translation from the Latin Vulgate, not from Hebrew and Greek. It was later authorized for use in America in 1810. It is still generally referred to as the Douai-Rheims Bible.

INDEPENDENT TRANSLATIONS

As well as attempted revisions of the AV/KJV, a number of entirely independent Protestant translations also appeared. A curious one was that of classical Greek scholar Edward Harwood, whose *Liberal Translation of the New Testament* (1768) had limited appeal: his rendering of the Lord's Prayer begins, "O thou great governour and parent of universal nature." Another private version was John Nelson Darby's *New Translation* (NT 1871; OT 1890). His New Testament had comprehensive footnotes detailing Greek manuscript evidence for the renderings he adopted. A founder of the Plymouth Brethren, he also made translations into German, French and Italian. His English translation is available today in some Bible software packages on CD-ROM. His work was consulted by those preparing the RV/ASV of 1885/1901 (see pp. 135-37).

In 1862, Robert Young, better known for his *Analytical Concordance*, published his *Literal Translation of the Bible*. The title is apt, for his translation is literal in the extreme, often retaining the Hebrew and Greek word order (see the example on p. 39). In particular, his method of translating Hebrew tenses makes his Old Testament in places virtually unreadable. A revised version appeared in 1898. Like J. N. Darby's work, it can also be found in CD-ROM packages.

Another literal translation was that of Joseph Rotherham. In *The Emphasized Bible* (NT 1872; OT 1897-1902), he employed special signs intended to capture the finer points of the original languages. Another notable feature is that he used "Yahweh" instead of "the LORD" throughout the Old Testament.

A more recent literal version in the same vein is *The Concordant Version of the Sacred Scriptures*, first published in 1926 and revised in 1931. It was edited by A. E. Knoch. An example of its utter incomprehensibility is found in 2 Corinthians 1:9-11: "But we have had the rescript of death in ourselves in order that we may be having no confidence in ourselves, but in God, Who rouses the dead, Who rescues us from a prodigious death, and will be rescuing, on Whom we rely, that He will still be rescuing also; you also assisting together by a petition for us, that from many faces He may be thanked for us by many, for our gracious gift."

AMERICAN TRANSLATIONS

Between the AV/KJV and the RV, a number of independent translations were published in America. The very first English Bible to be published in America was that of Charles Thomson in 1808. His Old Testament translation was made from the Greek Septuagint (see appendix one) rather than from the Hebrew, and his New Testament translation does not appear to take into account any Greek manuscripts discovered after the publication of the AV/KJV. Where his New Testament showed some novelty was in his translation of theological terms. "Gospel" becomes "glad tidings"; "repent" becomes "reform"; and "grace" becomes "favor." And in 1 Corinthians 13, "charity" becomes "love."

In 1833 dictionary maker Noah Webster published a revision of the AV/KJV in which he updated obsolete vocabulary. Many of his changes were incorporated in the RV/ASV (see below). The honor of being the first woman to translate the Bible into English goes to Julia E. Smith. Titled *The Holy Bible: Containing the Old and New Testaments; translated from the Original Tongues,* it was published in 1876 at her own expense.

THE REVISED VERSION (1885)

A further revision of the AV/KJV New Testament appeared in 1869, the work of Henry Alford, Dean of Canterbury Cathedral. He published it in the express hope of encouraging an authorized replacement for the whole AV/KJV. In February 1870, at a Convocation of the Church of England Province of Canterbury, a proposal was made to "report upon the desirableness of a revision of the Authorized Version of the New Testament." This proposal, made by Bishop Wilberforce of Winchester, was soon amended to include both Old and New Testaments.

The proposal was passed, and work began in June of that year. Representatives from the Church of Scotland and the Free Churches of both Scotland and England were invited to join the translation committee. Scholars from America were also invited but decided not to attend. Instead, it was agreed that an American edition would be published at a later date (see p. 137 on the ASV).

The New Testament was published in May 1881, the Old Testament in May 1885. The Apocrypha followed in 1895. F. F. Bruce writes, "The character of the two Testaments in the Revised Version presents such disparity in many ways that they must be considered sepa-rately."[1] In Bruce's opinion, the RV New Testament represents a great advance on the AV/KJV because the Greek text on which it rests is so much better. Two fourth-century Greek manuscripts had been discov-ered, *Codex Vaticanus* and *Codex Sinaiticus*, and were incorporated into a new Greek New Testament prepared by Cambridge scholars West-cott and Hort, both among the RV revisers.

Bruce goes on to say, however, that "with regard to the work of *translating* [his italics] the New Testament, the RV does lay itself open to criticism."[2] Partly because of their desire to retain one English word for one Greek word, a principle called "concordance," the RV reads a bit like a "schoolmasters' translation."[3] It is good for those who want a good base translation but not for those who want an attractive style for public reading. The great Baptist preacher Charles Haddon Spur-geon remarked that the RV New Testament was "strong in Greek, weak in English."[4]

As to the Old Testament, the revisers had before them the same un-derlying Hebrew text employed by the translators of the AV/KJV. It was not until well into the twentieth century that any new Hebrew manu-scripts came to light. What had improved in the interim, however, was the understanding of the Hebrew language. By the end of the nine-teenth century scholars were much clearer about the meaning of some rare Hebrew words. Commenting on the revisers' work, Bruce says, "In the poetical and prophetic books especially they helped English readers to understand the Old Testament as they had previously been unable to do."[5]

In addition to other changes, the RV was printed in paragraphs rather than having every verse beginning a new line as in the AV/KJV. There were also changes in punctuation and the use of italics. Chapter and page headings were omitted. A large number of alternative read-ings, however, were placed in the margins. In a highly critical review (1883) of the RV New Testament, the Dean of Winchester Cathedral, John William Burgon, said these simply bewildered readers and made them doubt the authority of Scripture.[6] Of particular concern to some was the removal of an entire verse, 1 John 5:7, which previously had been taken as a convenient proof-text for the doctrine of the Trinity. In the AV/KJV it reads: "For there are three that bear record in heaven, the Father, the Word, and the Holy Ghost: and these three are one." The Johannine Comma, as it is called, has no support from early manuscripts and does not now appear in modern translations except as a footnote (see p. 215).

The RV was produced in several editions, including some that set it alongside the text of the AV/KJV. Of particular value was an edition of 1898 containing very worthwhile marginal cross-references, taking the reader to other passages with verbal parallels, Old Testament quotations or a thematic connection. These form the basis of the cross-reference systems used over a century later in the ESV (pp. 187-92) and in a recent edition of the NRSV (pp. 170-72).

Although appreciated by scholars and initially received with some acclaim, the RV never threatened to replace the AV/KJV in popular use, either for private devotional reading or for church use. It was, however, a vital stepping-stone to further revisions in the Tyndale/KJV tradition, to which I shall return a little later.

THE AMERICAN STANDARD VERSION (1901)

Although British in origin, arguably the RV was greeted with more enthusiasm in America than on the British side of the Atlantic. On May 22, 1881, just two days after publication, two rival Chicago newspapers printed the RV New Testament in full. An American edition of the British RV was published (without the Apocrypha) in 1901 and is known as the American Standard Version (ASV). It is the basis of subsequent translations including the RSV (1952), the NASB (1971; updated 1995), and one Internet Bible, the WEB (p. 196).

The ASV incorporated some six hundred variants preferred by American scholars. Two significant preferences that run throughout the ASV are "Holy Spirit" (AV/KJV and RV: "Holy Ghost") and "Jehovah" (AV/KJV and RV: "the LORD"). It also shows some distinct improvements in style over the British edition.

EARLY TWENTIETH-CENTURY GROUNDBREAKERS

Neither the RV or its transatlantic counterpart, the ASV, had given the public a Bible in contemporary English. The style and language were still that of the AV/KJV. As the new century dawned, the need for a good modern-language Bible translation became increasingly apparent, and a number of new versions were forthcoming. Most of these were the work of just one or two individuals; it is not until the RSV (1952) that we see a return to cooperative committee translations.

The first modern-language version was published in 1901, with a thorough revision in 1904. *The Twentieth Century New Testament* was produced by a small British committee of volunteers drawn from a wide mix of backgrounds, though none of them specialists in New Testament Greek. Ahead of its time, it included modern paragraphing and punctuation (including direct speech in quotation marks) and units of measure given in their nearest English equivalent.

An early meaning-based translation, *The New Testament in Modern Speech* by public-school head and Greek scholar Richard Weymouth (1822-1902), was published posthumously in 1903. His translation was still popular in 1924, when a fourth revised edition was prepared by James Robertson. Weymouth's aim, in which he largely succeeded, was to produce a modern but dignified English rendering. His New Testament employs generally short sentences, especially in Paul's letters; modern punctuation, including quotation marks around direct speech; unobtrusive chapter and verse numbers; extensive footnotes; and the placing of Old Testament citations in capital letters.

The word *modern* appears in the titles of other early twentieth-century translations too. One such is *The Holy Bible in Modern English* by Ferrar Fenton (b. 1832). His New Testament was published in 1895, and the whole Bible in 1903. It remained in print until the 1940s. While his expressions have a certain forceful style, his work contains some distinctly idiosyncratic renderings. His translation of Genesis 1:1 incorporates the scientific views of his day: "By periods God created that which produced the Solar Systems; then that which produced the Earth."

Two further "modern-speech" versions, both from America, were *The Riverside New Testament*, first produced by William Ballantine in 1923 and revised in 1934, and the 1924 *Centenary Translation of the New Testament* by Helen Barrett Montgomery, which celebrated the hundredth anniversary of the American Baptist Publications Society. Montgomery's work is a rare example of a single-handed translation by a woman. Even in later cooperative committee translations, women are very poorly represented.

Better known and of more lasting influence was the work of Scottish divine James Moffatt (1870-1944). *The New Testament: A New Translation* was published in 1913, and *The Old Testament: A New Translation* in 1923. A one-volume edition followed in 1928. The first real competitor to Weymouth, it remains in print today.

F. F. Bruce says of Moffatt's work that it is "characterised by the freedom and vigour of his idiom. . . . Moffatt undoubtedly has made the Bible message intelligible, in spite of the detailed imperfections that may be found in his translation."[7] A particular feature of the first five books of the Old Testament is Moffatt's use of alternative typefaces to differentiate the various strands of writing supposedly underlying the text. Another feature is his use of "The Eternal" where the AV/KJV and other versions have "the LORD."

In Moffatt's later life, during which he lived in America, he served as a translator for the New Testament committee of the RSV. He also accepted an invitation to be its executive secretary for both the Old and the New Testament committees, a post he filled from 1937 until his death in June 1944.

The Complete Bible: An American Translation was the work of Edgar Goodspeed (NT 1923) and fellow University of Chicago professor J. M. Powis Smith (OT 1927), together with three assistants. A combined one-volume edition appeared in 1931, and the Apocrypha (translated by Goodspeed) was added in 1939. Goodspeed was among the first to translate *euangelion* ("gospel") as "Good News." Like Moffatt, Goodspeed also served on the New Testament committee of the RSV, as did Powis Smith until his death in 1932.

Yet another one-man translation effort was that of William Beck. He began translating the Bible in 1934, naming it *The Holy Bible: An American Translation* (not to be confused with Goodspeed's version of a similar name). Beck continued to work throughout the 1940s, 1950s and 1960s. His New Testament was published in 1963. He died in 1971 while working on the Old Testament, but this was completed on the basis of his notes, and the whole Bible was finally published in 1976 by Concordia Publishing. Beck's translation forms the basis of God's Word, a translation published in 1995 (see pp. 173-74). Beck was critical of the RSV when it appeared in 1952.

Two later one-man versions include Kenneth Taylor's Living Bible and Gerrit Verkuyl's Berkeley Version. The former, which became a mainstream version in its own right, will be discussed on pages 151-52. In 1945 Verkuyl produced a meaning-driven New Testament named after his home town in California "to bring us God's thoughts and ways in the language in which we think and live rather than that of our ancestors who expressed themselves differently." Verkuyl went on to oversee a similar translation of the Old Testament, prepared by some twenty scholars. His stated aim was to make a translation "less interpretive than Moffatt's, more cultured in language than Goodspeed's, more American than Weymouth's and freer from the King James Version than the Revised Standard." He largely succeeded; the Berkeley Version in Modern English, published in 1959,[8] was subsequently revised to become the Modern Language Bible in 1969. It can still be found, mostly in parallel editions of the New Testament.

Of the early twentieth-century translators, three stand out as having particular significance: Weymouth, Moffatt and Goodspeed. The work of all three can be described as "modern-speech" versions, even if none can be called a true meaning-driven translation. All break the mold of the AV/KJV and to an extent show a shift toward a meaning-driven approach. This approach did not have a well-thought-out basis in linguistic science at that time: the translators were acting more from intuition and a simple heartfelt desire to get the message of the Bible across in contemporary English.

Copies of all three are still sought after today and are valued by those who own them. Between them they prepared the way for the next era of Bible translation: an era that begins with the RSV, the first widely used modern English translation.

8

A NEW ERA BEGINS

Keep this book of the law on your lips. Recite it by day and by night,
that you may observe carefully all that is written in it; then you will
successfully attain your goal.

JOSHUA 1:8 NAB

⌘

None of the Bible translations discussed in the previous chapter ever seriously threatened the popularity and predominance of the AV/KJV. The RV and ASV, though appreciated for their scholarly improvements, lacked its rhythms and cadences and were deemed too excessively literal. And all the others were basically private one-person translations intended for personal use.

THE REVISED STANDARD VERSION (1952)

A new era in the history of English Bible translation began with the RSV, a Bible produced with widespread denominational support and not just by keen individuals. For Protestants, it was the first Bible to provide a real alternative to the AV/KJV. Looking at a copy now, the casual reader might be forgiven for wondering why the RSV of half a century ago was so much of a landmark: it stands firmly within the Tyndale/KJV tradition, it is still a form-driven translation, some of its pronouns are still archaic, and all of its language is still evidently biblish. But in its time the RSV was both highly significant and not a little controversial.

Sixteen years elapsed between the publication of the British RV and the ASV. In this interval, several unauthorized, Americanized editions of the RV appeared, so when the ASV was released, it was deemed prudent to safeguard it from tampering. It was copyrighted, and for the first time a Bible became intellectual property with vested financial interests—a significant factor in the development of the RSV and later translations. The copyright of almost all subsequent versions has been carefully protected.

In 1928 the copyright of the ASV was transferred to the International Council of Religious Education, a body linking together some forty denominations of the United States and Canada. The Council appointed the American Standard Bible Committee to take charge of the text and to consider a revision.

Although the Committee returned a positive recommendation just two years later, no funds for a revision were available until 1937, after the worst of the Depression years were over. Funding was made possible by an arrangement with publishers Thomas Nelson and Sons. In return for advance royalties, Nelson was given exclusive rights for a ten-year period after publication of the complete Bible.

Work began in 1938. The RSV New Testament was published in February 1946, and the Old Testament on September 30, 1952. Some three dozen scholars worked unpaid on the translation. After eighty-one meetings encompassing 450 twelve-hour working days, the complete RSV was launched with a massive publicity campaign. Nearly 3,500 celebration events were held in the United States, Canada and elsewhere, attended by an estimated 1.5 million people.

It had been hoped to include British scholars in the work of revision, but the war years made this impractical, and by the later stages some of the best British scholars were engaged in a fresh translation of their own, the New English Bible. The RSV did, however, receive a generally warm and positive welcome in Britain. In a broadcast review of the RSV, British scholar T. W. Manson said, "I like it because it is reliable and because it speaks directly to the man in the pew in the language he can reasonably be expected to understand."[1] It employed an English idiom without too many Americanisms, and a British-spelling edition was quickly introduced.

Most (though not all) of the AV/KJV archaisms were removed— "saith" became "says," and so on. The AV/KJV's trademark "And it came to pass" was gone. "Thee/thou" language also disappeared, except when divinity was being addressed. In this regard, the RSV received some criticism: Jesus was addressed as "you" in the Gospels in his earthly state, but as "thou" after the Ascension. The defense of the translators was that although Jesus remained divine in his incarnation, he was not thought of as such until after his exaltation. Unlike the ASV, but in line with the AV/KJV and the British RV, the RSV uses "the LORD," not "Jehovah," for the proper name of God in the Old Testament.

A few changes to the New Testament were made in 1952 when the Old Testament was published. Another eighty-five alterations, covering both Old and New Testaments, were made in 1962. One is of some theological interest: in Matthew 27:54 (and its parallel in Mark 15:39) the centurion's confession at the cross, "Truly this was a son of God," becomes "Truly, this was the Son of God."

An annotated edition, published by Oxford University Press, appeared in 1962, Nelson's sole publishing rights having expired. In 1971 a more major revision of the New Testament was forthcoming. Apart from other alterations, two disputed Gospel passages previously consigned to the footnotes were restored to the text, namely the longer ending of Mark (Mk 16:9-20) and the story of the woman caught in adultery (Jn 7:53—8:11), as well as some other shorter passages, mostly in Luke (see pp. 214-15).

One later high-selling edition of the RSV worthy of mention is the *Reader's Digest Bible* (North America 1982; Britain 1983). While all sixty-six books of the Bible are represented, this was an abridged edition: the Old Testament was shortened by half and the New Testament by a quarter. Similar editions appeared in other languages. An illustrated edition was issued in London in 1990. In 2002 Oxford University Press published special fiftieth anniversary editions.

The RSV sold particularly well until the late 1970s and still moderately well even after the NIV and other translations became available. Daniell reports that the RSV sold thirty million copies up to 1974 and a total of fifty-five million by the time the NRSV was released in 1990.[2]

Ecumenical. One intention behind the RSV was to provide an ecumenical Bible, one that might unite Christians of different theological and denominational persuasions. In practice, it proved both unifying and divisive.

Translation of the RSV Apocrypha was begun in 1953 and completed in 1957. Approaches from the Roman Catholic Church led to a Catholic edition of the New Testament being published in 1965 and the whole Bible, together with the deuterocanonical books and additions accepted by the Roman Church, in 1966. There were changes to some ninety-three verses in the New Testament prepared by the Catholic Biblical Association of Great Britain.[3]

In 1973 the RSV Common Bible was published and a copy presented to the Pope. This had four sections: the Old Testament, the deuterocanonical books and additions regarded as authoritative by Roman Catholics, the three remaining books of the Protestant Apocrypha not so regarded (namely *1-2 Esdras* and the *Prayer of Manasseh*), and the New Testament. These editions were helped by two developments within Catholicism: (1) a papal encyclical, *Divino Afflante Spiritu* (1943), encouraging the translation of the Bible from the original languages, not just the Latin Vulgate; and (2) the Second Vatican Council (1962-1965), which allowed cooperation with other denominations in developing Bible translations.

A further ecumenical development was made in 1977 with the addition of those books regarded as authoritative by the Eastern Orthodox Churches. A copy was presented to Dimitrios I, Ecumenical Patriarch of Constantinople. It has been described as the first truly ecumenical Bible in English.

Controversial. The RSV was regarded with suspicion by evangelicals, particularly the more conservative evangelicals of North America. Of the various features that met with criticism, none was more controversial than Isaiah 7:14. Where previous translations (in line with the New Testament in Mt 1:23) had stated that "a virgin shall conceive and bear a son," the RSV declared that "a young woman shall conceive"; "virgin" was consigned to a footnote. (See pp. 87-88 for a fuller explanation of this point.)

For some, this alone made the RSV a tool of the devil, but conservative evangelicals had other disagreements with the translators, too; among them

- the substitution of "expiation" for the earlier "propitiation" (Rom 3:25; Heb 2:17; 1 Jn 2:2; 4:10), arguably weakening the doctrine of the atonement (expiation means to blot out sin, while propitiation emphasizes the turning away of God's wrath)[4]

- the omission, on textual grounds, of "through his blood" in Colossians 1:14

- the omission altogether of the eunuch's response to the suggestion of baptism in Acts 8:37 (AV/KJV: "And Philip said, If thou believest with all thine heart, thou mayest. And he answered and said, I believe that Jesus Christ is the Son of God")

- the large number of conjectural readings in the Old Testament that depart from the standard Hebrew text

This was the era of Communist witch hunts, and some even suggested that the RSV had been inspired by "reds under the beds." A warning appeared in a 1960s U.S. Air Force training manual specifically cautioning recruits against the communist-tainted RSV. One pastor ceremonially burned a copy of the RSV with a blowtorch and sent the charred remains in a box to the translation committee. A senior translator, Bruce Metzger, comments, "That box, with its contents, is . . . a reminder that, though in previous centuries Bible translators were sometimes burned, today it is happily only a copy of the translation that meets such a fate."[5]

While some evangelicals dismissed the RSV out of hand, others saw potential in it. Luther Weigle, chairman of the RSV committee, was approached more than once about the possibility of producing an edition of the RSV more acceptable to conservatives. This was refused. The appearance of a Catholic edition rubbed salt in evangelical wounds and stiffened suspicion of the RSV and opposition to it still further. Out of this refusal the NIV was born (see pp. 159-62), and there has been an evangelical-ecumenical rift over the English Bible ever since, a rift that runs deeper in North America than in Britain.

THE AMPLIFIED BIBLE (1955)

The Amplified Bible is the production of the California not-for-profit Lockman Foundation. Originally published in parts (John's Gospel, 1954; NT, 1958; OT in two parts, 1952 and 1954), it was produced as a complete, one-volume Bible in 1955. It is "amplified" in the sense that additional bracketed words, together with various signs and punctuation marks, are placed in the text in order to bring out the full nuanced meaning of the original languages. John 3:16 becomes "For God so greatly loved *and* dearly prized the world that He [even] gave up His only-begotten (unique) Son, so that whoever believes in (trusts, clings to, relies on) Him shall not perish—come to destruction, be lost—but have eternal (everlasting) life."

While it is true that a word in Hebrew or Greek will have a range of meaning not always covered by just one word in English, it is wrong to assume the Hebrew or Greek word in question will carry that full range of meaning in every context. Generally, a writer has one specific meaning in mind when using a particular word. Reading the Amplified Bible is much like swallowing a thesaurus. It could not, with any intelligibility, be read aloud, but it does have some limited value for study purposes. For those with no knowledge of Hebrew or Greek, however, comparing two or three good modern translations is a far more effective way of getting at the meaning of the original.

THE NEW ENGLISH BIBLE (1970)

While North American scholars were working on the RSV, British scholars were working on a Bible of their own—not a revision, but an entirely fresh translation: the NEB.

In 1946 a proposal was put before the General Assembly of the

Church of Scotland that a new translation of the Bible be made "in the language of the present day." This decision was confirmed by a meeting of representatives of the Church of Scotland and the Church of England, together with Baptists, Congregationalists and Methodists. A Joint Committee was set up in January 1947. George Stuart Henry, the original proposer of the new translation, became the committee secretary. Further invitations were sent to other denominations in England, Wales and Ireland. Roman Catholics did not participate but did take up observer status in the later stages. The work was undertaken by four panels: one each for the Old and New Testaments and the Apocrypha, and a fourth giving advice on literary and stylistic questions. The author C. S. Lewis served on this final panel.

The New Testament appeared in 1961. Expectations were high. Wide media coverage brought long lines at bookstores. Four million copies were sold within the first year; seven million by the time the Old Testament and the Apocrypha appeared in 1970. Of these seven million, two-fifths were shipped to the United States; Americans apparently liked the quintessentially English style. The New Testament was revised in 1970 to coincide with the publication of the whole Bible. A study edition followed in 1976.

The NEB has three features in common with the RSV: the use of the most recently discovered manuscripts, including the Dead Sea Scrolls; the use of modern English except for the retention of "thee/thou" language when addressing God; and the large number of deviations from the standard Hebrew Old Testament text, for which both translations have been heavily criticized.[6] There, however, the similarities end. The RSV stands firmly in the Tyndale/KJV tradition and is a form-driven version; the NEB is distinctly different in style and a much freer translation. Metzger describes it thus: "A version marked by a vigorous and colourful English style, tending at places to be periphrastic with interpretive additions."[7]

The NEB is best described as highbrow and literary in style, though there is some unevenness, and here and there some peculiar idiosyncrasies, including the anachronism found in 1 Corinthians 16:8: "I will remain at Ephesus until Whitsuntide." Wycliffe, five centuries earlier, also had Whitsun for Pentecost.

The aim of the translators was not to replace the AV/KJV but to provide a Bible that people might use alongside the older version. It was widely used by private individuals, in schools, and as the pulpit Bible in many churches wanting to combine modernity with dignity. But arguably it was read more by those who did not attend church than by those who did.

Considerable thought was given to the presentation of the NEB. Prose was set in paragraphs, poetry as indented text. A single-column format was chosen over the traditional double-column layout, and verse numbers were consigned to the margin.[8]

The NEB was—and is—published jointly by the University Presses of Cambridge and Oxford. It has now been thoroughly updated, becoming in 1989 the Revised English Bible (see pp. 168-70).

Had there not been a nine-year gap between the Old and New Testaments, the NEB might have succeeded better than it did. As it was, by the 1970s it was losing much of its appeal and was soon overtaken by the translations that appeared later that decade. Its greatest achievement, however, was to be the first church-promoted Bible to break free from "Bible English" and to gain widespread acceptance among the general population.

THE NEW WORLD TRANSLATION (1961)

All the translations discussed in this book are used by Christian churches that hold to a trinitarian faith and to the full humanity and divinity of Christ. The one exception is the New World Translation (NWT) used by Jehovah's Witnesses and published by the Watchtower Bible and Tract Society. It is included simply because readers may have been shown a copy on their doorstep, as was I during a morning spent on the writing of this book.

The NWT New Testament appeared in 1950, the complete Bible in 1961. Revisions were made in 1970 and 1971. It generally aims to be "as literal as possible," but has certain distinctive features. The divine name

"Jehovah" is used throughout the Old Testament in preference to "God" or "the LORD." In the New Testament, certain passages have been translated in accordance with the Witnesses' beliefs. The best-known is John 1:1, which in the NWT states that the Word was "a god." Strictly speaking, this is a possible (though improbable) way of translating the Greek if the sentence is taken in isolation.[9] But of all four Gospels, none is clearer than John as to the eternal and divine nature of Christ. When the wider context of John's Gospel is borne in mind, the most natural rendering is the standard one: "And the Word was God."

The Witnesses also throw doubt on the divinity of the Spirit. In the trinitarian baptismal formula of Matthew 20:28, the NWT has "in the name of the Father and of the Son and of the holy spirit." The notes display a similar bias toward Watchtower teaching.

J. B. PHILLIPS'S NEW TESTAMENT (1958; REVISED 1972)

While serving as a wartime vicar in southeast London, John Bertram Phillips (1906-1982) published a paraphrase of Paul's letter to the Colossians in a parish magazine. He sent a copy to C. S. Lewis, who replied that it was "like seeing an old picture after it's been cleaned,"[10] and encouraged him to complete the New Testament. This appeared in parts:

- *Letters to Young Churches* (1947)
- *The Gospels in Modern English* (1952)
- *The Young Church in Action* [Acts] (1955)
- *The Book of Revelation* (1957)

A one-volume edition of the complete New Testament, *The New Testament in Modern English,* followed in 1958. Phillips undertook a full revision in 1972: it remains in print and, despite its male-oriented language, is still popular and read appreciatively.

Phillips himself and others have described his New Testament as a paraphrase. F. F. Bruce prefers to call it "a meaning-for-meaning translation."[11] Compared to later paraphrases such as Kenneth Taylor's Living Bible (see pp. 151-52) and Eugene Peterson's *The Message* (pp. 182-

83) or even translations such as the Contemporary English Version or the New Living Translation (pp. 174-78 and 178-81 respectively), Phillips's rendering is positively conservative. Paraphrase or translation, however, it is a work of true genius: the language is polished but accessible, simple but not simplistic. Two favorite verses of mine, which I long ago committed to memory, are James 1:2 ("When all kinds of trials and temptations crowd into your lives, my brothers, don't resent them as intruders, but welcome them as friends") and Romans 12:2:

> Don't let the world around you squeeze you into its own mould, but let God re-make you so that your whole attitude of mind is changed. Thus you will prove in practice that the will of God is good, acceptable to him and perfect.

Less well known than his New Testament is Phillips's *Four Prophets,* a rendering in similar style of the eighth-century-B.C. prophets Amos, Hosea, Isaiah (Phillips covers Is 1—39) and Micah, published in 1963. Sadly, while working on this project, Phillips experienced the onset of severe depression, something that was to plague him on and off for the rest of his life. It was, therefore, even more remarkable that in retirement he was able to complete a revision of his New Testament.

J. B. Phillips tells his own story in *Ring of Truth: A Translator's Testimony.* In it, he describes how his familiarity with the text and experience of translating it led him to uphold the reliability of Scripture at a time when many other scholars were growing increasingly skeptical.[12] Elsewhere, he described translating the Gospels as being "like rewiring the house with the mains switched on."[13]

THE LIVING BIBLE (1962-1971)

Kenneth Taylor had ten children. It was his habit to read them a section of the Bible as part of their family devotions, but he found they did not understand the ASV (1901) that he used. Beginning in 1956, Taylor used his forty-five-minute daily train journey to paraphrase passages of the ASV, which he would then read to his family that evening. His work was published stage by stage:

- *Living Letters* (1962)
- *Living Prophecies* (1965)
- *Living Gospels* (1966)
- *Living Psalms and Proverbs* (1967)

The New Testament was completed in 1967. More volumes followed:

- *Living Lessons of Life and Love* (1968)
- *Living Books of Moses* (1969)
- *Living History of Israel* (1970)

A complete one-volume Bible was published in 1971. By the mid-1970s, the LB accounted for almost half of all Bible sales in the United States. Taylor left his job at Moody Press in Chicago to set up his own company, Tyndale House Publishers. A British edition of the LB was forthcoming in 1974. In this, "clothes closet" becomes "wardrobe" (1 Sam 21:9), and 1 Samuel 24:3—which in the American edition tells us that "Saul went into the cave to go to the bathroom"—becomes "Saul went into the cave to relieve himself." A revision, the New Living Translation, appeared in 1996 (see pp. 178-81).

The LB makes no pretense at being a translation. It is a free paraphrase made without consulting the original languages. Its style is that of the street corner—chatty and conversational—and its reading level unlikely to make too many demands of even a young teenager. A few might find themselves shocked at some of the language. In 1 Samuel 20:30, in which King Saul calls Jonathan, "Thou son of the perverse rebellious woman" (ASV), Taylor opts for "You son of a bitch."

KNOX'S BIBLE (1945-1955)

A version of the Bible authorized, alongside the Douai-Rheims-Challoner, for Catholic use in Britain was that of Monsignor Ronald Knox (1888-1957). The New Testament was published in 1945, the Old Testament in two volumes in 1949, and the complete Bible as one volume in 1955.

Knox's aim was to put the Bible in words that an English person would naturally use to express the thoughts of the biblical writers. The Old Testament is considerably freer than the New. F. F. Bruce is full of praise for the results: "Knox's version has the overwhelming advantage of being the work of a man who had an uncanny instinct for getting the right word or the right phrase in any given context. . . . Knox was a master of English style. . . . Never did a translation read less like a translation."[14]

From a scholar's viewpoint, however, Knox's work is disadvantaged by being a translation not from the Old Testament Hebrew and the New Testament Greek but from the Latin Vulgate. Although a considerable improvement on Douai-Rheims-Challoner, it was soon superseded by the Catholic edition of the RSV (1966) and the JB (also 1966).

THE JERUSALEM BIBLE (1966)

In 1948, a group of French Dominican monks working at L'École Biblique et Archéologique Française in Jerusalem produced a series of Bible commentaries, complete with a French translation of the whole Bible. In 1956 this was issued as a study Bible with the commentary condensed into footnotes and introductions to each book of the Bible. This in turn was translated into English by twenty members of the British Catholic Biblical Association and was published as the Jerusalem Bible in 1966.

The JB lays claim to being the first complete Catholic Bible to be translated into English from Hebrew and Greek instead of from the Latin Vulgate. While this is true, the significant influence of the French version cannot be overlooked. A few books, the preface admits, were translated from the French and only then compared to the Hebrew and Greek. The study notes were translated directly from the French. One of the stylistic consultants was J. R. R. Tolkien, famed author of *The Lord of the Rings*.

The translation is more meaning-driven than form-driven, but only barely so. Only occasionally is there evidence of interpretive phrasing. The language has a contemporary ring to it but remains sufficiently dignified for liturgical use. One noticeable feature of the JB is the rendering of the divine name as "Yahweh." Isaiah 7:14, which proved so controversial for the RSV, becomes "The maiden is with child," a clever compromise.

Being a Catholic Bible, the deuterocanonical writings are included in their preferred Catholic positions. Although editions with and without the study notes were made available, the great value of the JB lies in the high-quality scholarship of the notes and cross-references. Many Protestants have been drawn to the JB for this reason and because of the suitability of its style for public reading. The preface suggests that those reading aloud from the JB may want to substitute "the LORD" for "Yahweh," the latter being strange to many ears.

An edition of the Psalms based on the JB appeared in 1963. This, the Grail Translation, was intended for liturgical use. An inclusive-language edition followed in 1983 and was further revised in 1995. In the Grail, "LORD" is used rather than "Yahweh." The JB was superseded by the New Jerusalem Bible in 1985 (see pp. 164-65).

THE NEW AMERICAN BIBLE (1970)

While the JB and its successor became the standard modern Bible for Catholic use in Britain, in America that honor goes to the New American Bible (not to be confused with the New American Standard Bible).

The NAB began life as the Confraternity Version. In 1941 the Catholic Biblical Association of America, sponsored by the Episcopal Confraternity of Christian Doctrine, completed a revision of the Douai-Rheims New Testament, prepared from the Latin Vulgate but with some reference to the Greek. The Old Testament followed in four volumes between 1952 and 1959. Coming after Pope Pius XII's encyclical *Divino Afflante Spiritu* in 1943, which approved translation from the original languages, this was made from the Hebrew Bible, not the Vulgate.

Following the Second Vatican Council (1962-1965), the Confraternity authorized a further translation. In 1970 an entirely new New Testament was completed, this time from the Greek, and was published alongside a small-scale revision of the Confraternity Old Testament.

Among other changes from the Confraternity Version, the NAB finally abandoned "thee/thou" language and replaced peculiarly Catholic spellings of proper names with those in general use (e.g., Isaiah for Isaia and Malachi for Malachia).

Metzger praises parts of the NAB, such as the book of Psalms, which he says "gives the impression that meticulous care was taken to provide a rendering with a certain liturgical and literary timbre. In general the language is dignified without being archaic, and expressions are used that evoke a sense of grandeur and the numinous." He is more critical of other parts of the Bible, in which "the reader is struck by a certain typically American quality of English idiom—plain, flat, and matter-of-fact. . . . One can point out a number of rather uninspired, pedestrian renderings."[15]

A further revision of the NAB, now the Bible most widely used by American Catholics, is underway, partly for the purpose of introducing inclusive language. The revised New Testament and Psalms appeared in 1986. One can detect a move in the direction of a more form-driven translation style as well as a general improvement of previous, somewhat slipshod renderings that escaped notice in an otherwise good translation. A number of Catholic study editions are available.

FORMATIVE YEARS

THE 1970S AND 1980S

Christ's message in all its richness must live in your hearts.

COLOSSIANS 3:16 TEV

From the early 1970s on, the pace of new translations has increased rapidly. This chapter considers the origins of some of the most popular translations.

THE NEW AMERICAN STANDARD BIBLE (1971)

Because of suspicions relating to the RSV, there was a continuing demand for a form-driven evangelical translation. In 1959, the Lockman Foundation (which had already produced the Amplified Bible) began work on its own revision of the ASV, the copyright of which had expired. The work of some sixty originally anonymous translators, the complete NASB was published in 1971, with earlier releases of the Gospel of John in 1960, the other Gospels in 1962, and the New Testament in 1963.

The NASB is a literal translation, far more so than the AV/KJV to the point of being wooden. It is considerably more form-driven than even the RSV, and in the Old Testament far more firmly rejects any conjectural readings or deviations from the traditionally accepted Hebrew text. Its more obvious literary features are

- retention of "thee/thou" language in prayer to God
- retention of italics for words supplied to make sense in English (as in the AV/KJV)
- every verse beginning a new line (like the AV/KJV)
- a careful distinction of Greek tenses in the New Testament
- "the LORD" instead of the ASV's "Jehovah"
- capitalization of pronouns relating to God, Jesus Christ or the Holy Spirit
- printing New Testament quotations of the Old Testament entirely in small capitals

In addition, one of the NASB's most attractive study features, found in some editions, is its highly regarded cross-reference system.

By 1977, the NASB was the best-selling modern Bible in America, but it was overtaken by the NIV after the latter was published in 1978. Even since then, the NASB has maintained a degree of popularity among conservative evangelicals in the United States for its literal rendering of the original languages. In Britain, the NASB had a relatively short spell of popularity in certain circles in the early 1970s but was rapidly ousted by the TEV and the NIV. An updated NASB appeared in 1995 (see p. 173), which has revived its popularity, certainly in North America. While useful for study purposes, the NASB cannot easily be recommended for public reading or liturgical use.

Two translations, each with an enduring worldwide popularity, were both groundbreaking in different ways. By the end of the twentieth century, one of them would cause as much controversy as did the RSV in mid-century.

TODAY'S ENGLISH VERSION (1976)

The TEV was the first thoroughgoing meaning-driven translation. The principles behind it were directly derived from the work of Eugene Nida and his experience in mission-field translation for first-time Bible readers (see chaps. 1-2 for a full discussion of these principles).

The original aim in producing the TEV was to meet the needs of those for whom English was a second language, but it immediately proved popular among native English speakers too, especially children and young people. The language of the TEV is natural, clear, simple and unambiguous. Cultural words (such as *centurion*) have been modernized, as have doctrinal terms such as *justification*. The style is conversational English and the reading level relatively easy—suited to a ten-year-old reader.

The TEV New Testament was the work of one man, Robert Bratcher, a former Southern Baptist missionary commissioned by the American Bible Society for the task. It appeared in 1966 under the now archaic-sounding title *Good News for Modern Man*. It quickly sold twelve million copies. A group of seven translated the Old Testament, which was published along with revisions to the New Testament in 1976. A novel feature of the TEV was the inclusion of Swiss artist Annie Vallotton's simple line-drawings, giving an attractive appearance to the page and helping to break up otherwise solid text.

The TEV has been accused of being overinterpretive, even a paraphrase, especially in places where it attempts to make implicit information explicit and where it turns figurative and poetic language into plain prose. In 1 Samuel 20:30, where the LB has Saul call Jonathan "You son of a bitch," the TEV is even more terse: "You bastard!"

Both American- and British-spelling editions of the TEV were made available. An edition with the Apocrypha was introduced in 1979 to meet the needs of Roman Catholic schools. An inclusive-language edition was published in 1992 (1994 in Britain). However, the number of changes was relatively small, averaging only two or three a page. The new edition was introduced with little fanfare or fuss.

The TEV continues to be popular, especially as a children's Bible, despite showing some signs of becoming dated and despite the arrival of the CEV (see pp. 174-78), which was designed to replace it. American readers have shown a preference for the LB (see pp. 151-52), but in Britain sales figures and surveys suggest that until the mid-1980s the TEV was equal in popularity to the NIV.

THE NEW INTERNATIONAL VERSION (1978)

The third edition of F. F. Bruce's *History of the English Bible*, long regarded as the standard work on English translations, was published in 1979. The NEB merits a whole chapter, the TEV gets five pages, but the NIV gets less than a single page. In an early 1975 review of the NIV New Testament, Sakae Kubo and Walter Specht dared to suggest that the NIV, when complete, would "probably be used widely as the Bible for conservative Christians."[1] A prophetic understatement indeed: for almost twenty years now it has been the world's most popular Bible, outselling even the AV/KJV.

As early as 1953 two separate inquiries about publishing an evangelical edition of the RSV were declined.[2] Separately from this, in 1955, Christian businessman Howard Long asked the Christian Reformed Church (CRC), of which he was a member, to consider the need for a Bible suited to evangelistic work. In 1956 the Synod of the CRC appointed a committee to consider the possibility. The National Association of Evangelicals independently set up a similar inquiry in 1957. A joint committee of the two groups was formed in 1961.

In a two-hour meeting in 1966 with Luther Weigle, chairman of the RSV committee, the option of preparing an evangelical edition of the RSV was again refused, despite the appearance of a Catholic edition in the same year. Other translations, including the Berkeley Version (see p. 140) and the as-yet-incomplete New American Standard Bible (pp. 156-57) were also deemed unsuitable for what was in mind. So work on the NIV began in 1967, undertaken by the New York Bible Society (subsequently renamed the International Bible Society and relocated to Colorado Springs).

The NIV New Testament was published in the fall of 1973 (with a sampler edition of John's Gospel appearing earlier in 1969) and the complete Bible on October 27, 1978 (with prior samplers of Isaiah, Daniel, Proverbs and Ecclesiastes). A Commonwealth Edition New Testament with British spelling and idiom came in 1973, and the complete Bible in 1979. The principal American publisher remains Zondervan, while Hodder & Stoughton publishes the British edition.

Although not in the Tyndale/KJV style, the NIV is not as far removed from it as its contemporary, the TEV. The English of the NIV is more formal and less conversational than that of the TEV. Unlike the RSV and NASB, the NIV nowhere employs "thee/thou" language and is not a revision of an earlier translation. Soon after the release of the NT, Kubo and Specht offered this comparison with some of the NIV's contemporaries: "The NIV translation is accurate and clear. It does not have the color or striking characteristics of Phillips or the NEB but it is dependable and straightforward. It is more modern than the RSV and less free than the NEB or Phillips."[3]

In more recent advertising, the NIV translators declared it to be a translation that strives for a balance between accuracy, beauty, clarity and dignity. The translation philosophy of the NIV stands on the border between meaning-driven and form-driven approaches. The translators put it thus:

> As for the NIV, its method is an eclectic one with the emphasis for the most part on a flexible use of concordance and equivalence, but with a minimum of literalism, paraphrase, or outright dynamic equivalence. In other words, the NIV stands on middle ground—by no means the easiest position to occupy. It may fairly be said that the translators were convinced that, through long patience in seeking the right words, it is possible to attain a high degree of faithfulness in putting into clear and idiomatic English what the Hebrew and Greek texts say.[4]

The NIV is very much a committee translation, including scholars from many parts of the English-speaking world—eighty-seven from the United States, three each from Britain and Canada, and two each from Australia and New Zealand make up one of the largest teams ever assembled for any translation.

A smaller, fifteen-member team forms the permanent Committee on Bible Translation (CBT). As described in the translation's preface, all the translators, although from a wide variety of denominations, have subscribed to "the authority and infallibility of Scripture of the

Bible as God's Word in written form." The NIV restored "virgin" to Isaiah 7:14 and has "atoning sacrifice" for the RSV's "expiation" (AV/KJV and ESV have "propitiation," but NRSV has "atoning sacrifice").

The CBT's executive secretary, Edwin Palmer (1922-1980), was succeeded by Kenneth Barker, who also served as editor of the very successful *NIV Study Bible*, first published in 1985 (1987 in the U.K.). On publication of the complete Bible in 1978, some revisions were made to the New Testament. A further 930 minor amendments were introduced in 1984. The 1984 edition has remained the standard NIV text to date.

Balance is an NIV keyword. Indeed, a whole book, Kenneth Barker's *The Balance of the NIV,* has been dedicated to praising it as a balanced translation. This is both its strength and perhaps its weakness. For many, the NIV is the ideal, all-around translation, suitable for devotional use, study purposes and public reading. But like anything that positions itself as a middle-of-the-road product, it is open to being shot at from all sides. The NIV has been picked over more closely than probably any other translation in history.

From the late 1980s to the present, there has been something of a backlash against the principle of meaning-driven translation and a trend (or at least a loud campaign) favoring form-driven versions. Much of the criticism has come from those who do not believe the NIV to be literal enough. Many of these stand in the KJV-only camp, arguing that only a word-for-word translation fits with their understanding of the verbal inspiration of Scripture.

A more moderate but persistent critic of the NIV has been Robert Martin, who argues that it is the task of the preacher and the commentator, not the translator, to explain Scripture. His book *Accuracy of Translation*[5] takes the NIV to task in places where it employs a meaning-driven rather than a form-driven approach. Martin makes a cogent argument for the latter philosophy, but to be fair to the NIV, it never claims to be a word-for-word translation. It does, of course, quite naturally claim to be accurate. Martin's points are rebutted by Barker in his book *Accuracy Defined and Illustrated.*[6]

Over the years, the NIV has had proponents and opponents, but its success cannot be denied. Depending on which statistics one reads and believes, the NIV became the most popular Bible, outselling even the AV/KJV, at some point between 1986 and 1988. Twenty-five years after its first publication, over 110 million copies of the NIV were in print, compared with estimated total sales for the AV/KJV of 300 million since 1611. Compared to the RSV, the NIV sold twice as many copies in half the time. Prior to the inclusive-language controversy discussed in chapter eleven, a massive 45 percent of all Bibles sold in North America were NIV translations. There are also editions in Spanish, French and Portuguese.

THE NEW KING JAMES VERSION (1982)

Several attempts have been made to modernize the AV/KJV. The most popular is the NKJV. In it "thee/thou" language has been updated, and archaic words and expressions replaced. Many of the words and phrases that appear in italics in the AV/KJV—added to make better English sense—are omitted. Personal pronouns referring to God are capitalized. The work of Art Farstad (d. 1998), the NKJV New Testament rests on the same underlying Greek text as used in 1611 for the AV/KJV.

Two popular study Bibles, both published in 1997, are based on the NKJV: the *MacArthur Study Bible* and the *Nelson Study Bible*. Both reflect the conservative scholarship appreciated by readers of this Bible. In Britain, the NKJV is sometimes referred to as the Revised Authorized Version. In recent years, the popularity of the NKJV in the United States has been exceeded only by the NIV and AV/KJV, due largely to high profile advertising and door-to-door selling.

Steven Sheeley and Robert Nash, however, are damning in their review of the NKJV:

> The NKJV is open to one of the most devastating criticisms levelled at the KJV, without being able to point to limitations of history and language. The KJV translators had little choice but to use the majority or "received" text in 1611; most of the earlier manuscripts lay as yet undiscovered. Given their academic excellence and deep reverence for the Bible, one would suppose that they

would use the best text available, no matter what difficulties it posed. Any "reverence" for the text in the NKJV, however, seems to be for the English text of the KJV, rather than for the ancient texts of the Bible.

The translation itself does little more than update the language of the KJV. Archaic forms . . . have been eliminated in favour of more modern speech patterns. Places where the KJV is known to be inaccurate in its grammar and idiom have been corrected and smoothed over. Even in this, however, the NKJV has been criticized for producing a text with language that was never really used by any generation of English-speaking people. It is a curious combination of the old and the new: a new patch on an old garment.[7]

Table 9.1 gives a comparison of Romans 3:21-26 in the AV/KJV and NKJV (table 1.3 compares the same passage in the NASB and the CEV). Other attempts to update the AV/KJV are listed in appendix two.

Table 9.1. Romans 3:21-26 in the AV/KJV and NKJV (Italics in the Originals)

AV/KJV (1611)	NKJV (1982)
[21]But now the righteousness of God without the law is manifested, being witnessed by the law and the prophets; [22]Even the righteousness of God *which is* by faith of Jesus Christ unto all and upon all them that believe: for there is no difference: [23]For all have sinned, and come short of the glory of God; [24]Being justified freely by his grace through the redemption that is in Christ Jesus: [25]Whom God hath set forth *to be* a propitiation through faith in his blood, to declare his righteousness for the remission of sins that are past, through the forbearance of God; [26]To declare, *I say,* at this time his righteousness: that he might be just and the justifier of him which believeth in Jesus.	[21]But now the righteousness of God without the law is revealed, being witnessed by the law and the prophets, [22]even the righteousness of God, through faith in Jesus Christ, to all and on all who believe. For there is no difference: [23]for all have sinned, and come short of the glory of God; [24]being justified freely by His grace through the redemption that is in Christ Jesus, [25]whom God set forth *as* a propitiation by His blood, through faith, to demonstrate His righteousness, because in His forbearance God had passed over for the sins that were previously committed, [26]to demonstrate at the present time His righteousness, that He might be just, and the justifier of the one who has faith in Jesus.

THE NEW JERUSALEM BIBLE (1985)

Although the English JB was published in 1966 (see pp. 153-54), the French translation on which it rested and its study notes were another decade older. A new edition of the French work appeared in 1973, incorporating widespread changes to both biblical text and notes. This warranted a revision of the English edition: the NJB was published in 1985.

The NJB, unlike parts of its predecessor, was made entirely from the Hebrew and Greek, with very little reference to the French. The foreword, written by general editor Dom Henry Wansborough (now deceased) of Ampleforth Abbey, Yorkshire, explains other changes, revealing the NJB to be more of a form-driven translation than the JB, while also incorporating some acceptance of inclusive language:

> The character of the *Jerusalem Bible* as primarily a study Bible has been a prime consideration. Paraphrase has been avoided more rigorously than in the first edition; care has been taken that in parallel passages (for example in the first three gospels) the similarities and differences should be mirrored exactly in the translation. Key terms in the original, especially those theological key concepts on which there is a major theological note, have been rendered throughout (with very few exceptions) by the same English word, instead of by a variety of words used in the first edition.
>
> At the same time the widespread liturgical use of this version has been taken into account; while it is hoped that the translation is fresh and lively, care has been taken to reproduce the dignity of the originals by a certain measured phrasing and avoidance of the colloquial.
>
> Considerable efforts have been made, though not at all costs, to soften or avoid the inbuilt preference of the English language, a preference now found so offensive by some people, for the masculine; the word of the Lord concerns men and women equally.

The NJB, like the JB, continues to employ "Yahweh" where other versions have "the LORD." Where in the Beatitudes (Mt 5:3-10) the JB had "Happy," the NJB reverts to the more traditional "Blessed." Isaiah 7:14 has "young woman" (the JB had "maiden") in preference to "virgin."

THE NEW CENTURY VERSION (1991); THE INTERNATIONAL CHILDREN'S BIBLE (1986)

Two closely related translations are the NCV and the ICB. Often children's Bibles are derived from adult versions; the vocabulary is simplified and sentences shortened. With these two Bibles it is the other way around.

Both Bibles are derivative of a Bible prepared for the deaf, a project of the World Bible Translation Center based in Fort Worth, Texas. The New Testament was completed in 1978 and published by Baker Book House as the *English Version for the Deaf*. In 1980 it was offered to a wider audience under the title *A New Easy-to-Read Version*. Revisions were made over the next few years and published by Sweet Publishing in two different covers, aimed respectively at children (ICB) and adults (NCV). The Old Testament was completed in 1986.

Although bearing distinct titles, there was no real difference between the text of the two until a more substantial revision was made in 1991, by which time Sweet Publishing had been acquired by Word. The adult edition was revised, giving the NCV a higher reading level than the ICB. Both are now published by Nelson Word. The NCV has longer sentences, has a slightly more sophisticated vocabulary, and is somewhat less choppy than the ICB. Where the ICB has a reading age of 9 years, the NCV scores 10.3 years.

Both the ICB and NCV are thoroughgoing meaning-driven translations, but not to the same extent as, say, the TEV or CEV. The NCV employs inclusive language; the ICB does not. The NCV is particularly popular among teenagers and young people, for whom several special editions are available. The ICB is the only complete Bible translation (as opposed to children's story Bibles) specifically prepared for preteen children.

THE CHRISTIAN COMMUNITY BIBLE (1988)

Out of pastoral concern for the poor Chilean Christian communities among which he worked, French Catholic priest Bernardo Hurault prepared a translation in Spanish, together with study notes answering the questions the peasant Christians were raising with him. He worked alone on an old portable typewriter. At one point he had to sell his typewriter to buy food but continued his efforts by hand. Eventually, his work received official recognition by the Catholic churches of various Latin American countries and financial support from Spain.

Father Hurault then went to Asia, overseeing versions of his Bible in several more languages. In the Philippines, he lived among the poorest of the poor, where he met Alberto Rossa, a priest engaged in spreading the gospel through publishing. Rossa convinced Hurault that an English-language version was necessary. At the age of sixty, Hurault hurriedly learned English and spent just eighteen months, helped by a team of scholars, theologians and poets, producing the English CCB.

The CCB is a translation from the original languages, employing reasonably straightforward language but claiming a high degree of accuracy. It is not dissimilar to the NIV in reading level and in its balance between meaning-driven and form-driven approaches, though it is less consistent in English style. Inclusive language is used throughout. The notes and book introductions are of a liberal Catholic outlook. It has proved popular in the Republic of Ireland.

There are some oddities to the CCB. In some books of the Old Testament, "Yahweh" is used in reference to God; in others, "the LORD" is used. Passages deemed to be less important are printed in smaller type, a device found in some early British editions of the CEV. Additionally, the Old Testament books are arranged in an unorthodox order.

The CCB had its origins in Latin America and remains unknown to many English-speaking readers. Nevertheless, it deserves mention, not least because of the remarkable story of its dissemination. It continues to be published from the Philippines, but the most recent editions, including two Chinese versions, are printed in mainland China, something unthinkable just a few years ago. At the time of writing, the CCB is available in twelve languages and is being prepared in eleven more. The Spanish edition alone claims sales of forty million.

10

OLD FACES
IN NEW GUISES

Flowers and grass will fade away,

but what our God has said

will never change.

ISAIAH 40:8 CEV

☙

From the late 1980s to the present, the story of the English Bible is the story of revision as much as it is of newcomers. Of the sixteen versions reviewed in this chapter and the next, eleven are revisions or replacements; only five are new. Only one is a British contribution; the remainder are all American.

THE REVISED ENGLISH BIBLE (1989)

The NEB was completed in 1970; just three years later a decision was made to revise it. The NEB had been conceived just after the Second World War and was nearly out of date by the time it was finished. In the same year that the NEB was completed, the Church of England approved new forms of worship that moved away from the traditional language of the Prayer Book. "Thee/thou" language, retained in the NEB for addressing God, began to disappear from public worship and private prayer.

Also in the early 1970s, the charismatic movement and improvements in sound technology, began to have an impact on the worship style of many churches, whether themselves charismatic or not. Informality became the order of the day. The NEB, with its highbrow literary style, did not suit these changes and quickly started to look dated.

The director of the revision was W. D. McHardy, who had overseen the translation of the NEB Apocrypha. Chairing the Joint Committee was Donald Coggan, Archbishop of Canterbury from 1974 to 1980. The Roman Catholic Church, which had taken observer status in the latter stages of work on the NEB, became a full member of the new committee. And entirely new to the committee were representatives of the Moravian Churches and the Salvation Army.

The REB largely retains the style of the NEB but is a substantial and much improved revision. More obvious differences include

- the removal of all "thee/thou" language
- some minor concessions to inclusive language ("brothers" becomes "brothers and sisters")
- Slightly less bookish language and fewer convoluted sentences
- fewer idiosyncratic renderings, such as Joshua 15:18 (NEB "she broke wind"; REB "she dismounted") and the Greek word *ekklēsia* (NEB varies between "church," "congregation," "community" and "the meeting"; REB is consistently translated "church")
- fewer speculative, conjectural readings in Old Testament passages; more readings were taken from the Hebrew Masoretic Text and fewer from the Greek Septuagint (see appendix one for an explanation of these text matters)
- the reintroduction of the traditional Hebrew headings in the Psalms
- a larger number of section headings

It was hoped to complete the revision within seven years, but the REB was not published until September 1989, jointly by the University Presses of Oxford and Cambridge,[1] with the Old Testament, Apocrypha and New Testament appearing simultaneously. As with the NEB before it, the excessive length of time from conception to birth has been the downfall of the REB. The 1970s and 1980s saw the advent of several translations, such as the TEV and the NIV, with which the REB could never hope to compete in popularity. However, it deserves to be better known and more widely used than it is. It can be praised for its clarity when read aloud.

THE NEW REVISED STANDARD VERSION (1990)

In the light of further fragments from the Dead Sea and early Greek papyrus manuscripts being made available to scholars, the National Council of Churches of Christ of the USA in 1974 invited the committee that had oversight of the RSV to commence a further revision. A fourfold mandate was set out:

1. to improve paragraph structure and punctuation
2. to eliminate archaisms, including all "thee/thou" language
3. to improve accuracy, clarity and English style, especially when read aloud
4. to eliminate masculine-oriented language (though not with reference to God)

As with many planned revisions, the work resulted in a far more extensive updating than first intended. Table 10.1 shows some comparisons to illustrate the changes.[2]

The translation philosophy of the NRSV, like other translations in the Tyndale/KJV tradition, is unmistakably form-driven. Its guiding principle is "as literal as possible, as free as necessary." It is perhaps the most thoroughgoing of all translations in its deployment of gender-inclusive language. Some would argue that this runs counter to the principle of literal translation.

Mark Strauss, otherwise a defender of inclusive language and an informal adviser to the Today's New International Version in this regard (see pp. 186-87), criticizes the NRSV for occasions where the translators exceed their mandate and employ inclusive language even when it is clear that only males are intended.[3] An example is Proverbs, a book that contains advice given by a father to his son. The NRSV changes "My son" to "My child" throughout. Another is Titus 1:5-6, where the

Table 10.1. Revisions from the RSV to the NRSV

Passage	RSV (1952)	NRSV (1990)	Nature of change
Deut 29:5	Your sandals have not worn off your feet.	The sandals on your feet have not worn out.	More intelligible
Ps 39:9	I am dumb.	I am silent.	Less ambiguous
Amos 6:5	. . . like David invent for themselves instruments of music	. . . like David improvise on instruments of music	More accurate
Zech 3:3	Now Joshua was standing before the angel, clothed in filthy garments.	Now Joshua was dressed with filthy clothes as he stood before the angel.	Clearer English
Lk 22:35	"Did you lack anything?" They said "Nothing."	"Did you lack anything?" They said, "No, not a thing."	Clearer when read aloud
2 Cor 11:25	Once I was stoned.	Once I received a stoning.	Less ambiguous
Eph 3:16	. . . grant you to be strengthened with might by his Spirit in the inner man	. . . grant that you may be strengthened in your inner being with power through his Spirit	More inclusive
Rev 2:29	He who has an ear, let him hear what the Spirit says to the churches.	Let anyone who has an ear listen to what the Spirit is saying to the churches.	More inclusive

Greek says that elders must be "the husband of but one wife" (RSV); the NRSV says they must be "married only once." Strauss also dislikes the NRSV's overuse of the neologism *humankind* as a replacement for *man*.[4]

Like the RSV before it, the NRSV has sought widespread denominational acceptance. Editions with the Apocrypha contain those books deemed deuterocanonical by the Roman Catholic Church as well as those used by the Eastern Orthodox Churches.

Bruce Metzger of Princeton Theological Seminary supervised the translation committees. An anglicized edition of the NRSV was undertaken by Roger Coleman, stylistic adviser and coordinating secretary for the REB, and was published by Oxford University Press in 1995. A cross-reference edition of the anglicized NRSV, published by Oxford University Press in 2003 and available with or without the Apocrypha, is one of the best cross-reference Bibles in print.

The NRSV has won widespread acceptance as a scholarly translation suitable for both study and liturgical use. While some conservatives have retained their suspicions over the theological pedigree of the NRSV (like the RSV, it has "young woman," not "virgin," in Is 7:14), it is the standard Bible in many theological colleges and university divinity departments and is replacing other translations as the preferred basis for biblical commentaries and study Bibles. At least six million copies of the NRSV have been sold since publication.

THE NEW TESTAMENT AND PSALMS: AN INCLUSIVE VERSION (1995)

In 1995 Oxford University Press published an American adaptation of the NRSV, *The New Testament and Psalms: An Inclusive Version*. Dubbed the "Politically Correct Bible" by critics, this adaptation of the NRSV went far beyond the bounds of legitimate translation methods, taking the notion of an inclusive Bible to new heights—or, depending on one's perspective, new depths. Its avowed aim is to

> replace or rephrase all gender-specific language not referring to particular historical individuals, all pejorative references to race, color or religion, and all identifications of persons by their physical disability alone, by means of paraphrase, alternative renderings, and other acceptable means of conforming the language of the work to an inclusive idea.

So, in the NTPI "lepers" become "people with leprosy" and "slaves" become "enslaved persons." God becomes our "Father-Mother," and

Jesus now sits "near to God" because, apparently, to suggest that he sits "at God's right hand" might offend those who are left-handed. And not wanting to offend people of color, one sits not in "darkness" but in "captivity." The "Son of Man" becomes the "Human One," "kings" become "rulers" and so forth. This is more than translation: ignoring the Bible's historical and cultural background, this is a rewriting of the biblical text.

THE NEW AMERICAN STANDARD BIBLE UPDATE (1995)

The NASB first appeared in 1971 (see pp. 156-57). Like the RSV, NEB and JB, it retained "thee/thou" language when referring to God. Its 1995 update removes all archaic language, which is its most immediately noticeable difference from the original NASB. But there are other changes too. Some vocabulary has been updated (e.g., "chest" for "breast" and "sash" for "girdle" in the description of the glorified Christ in Rev 1:13), awkward English is smoothed out, and difficult word order is corrected. Fewer sentences start with *And*. Other changes relate to textual issues and bringing parallel passages into line. No concessions, however, have been made to inclusive language.

The NASBu is available in two printed formats: either with every verse beginning a new line or with full paragraphing. The original NASB remains in print, and both are widely available in a variety of electronic formats. Like its predecessor, the NASBu will be appreciated by those who want a literal translation for study purposes (its cross-referencing system is among the best), but it is still too wooden to serve most churches as a pulpit or pew Bible.

GOD'S WORD (1995)

The 1995 God's Word translation eschews both a rigid form-driven approach and too loose a meaning-driven philosophy. Striving for what it calls in its preface "closest natural equivalence," it seeks "to avoid the awkwardness and inaccuracy associated with form-equivalent translation and to avoid the loss of meaning and oversimplification associated with function-equivalent translation."

This lesser-known translation is published by God's Word to the

Nations Bible Society, an American Lutheran organization with a concern for world mission. Their translation employs a single-column format, well-laid out poetry, gender-inclusive language, generally short sentences and, where possible, nontheological vocabulary. Any theological words that are retained are explained in footnotes. While the English is clear, it is perhaps a little bland. The reading level of God's Word is on a par with Bibles often used by children and youth, such as the CEV and NCV (see pp. 174-78; 165).

Despite its claim to be so, God's Word is not an entirely new translation. It was previously titled the New Evangelical Translation (1988, revised 1992) and is actually modeled on the earlier work of William Beck (see p. 140).

THE NEW INTERNATIONAL READER'S VERSION (1994-1998)

The NIrV is a simplified revision of the NIV with shorter sentences and easier vocabulary. The history of the NIrV is entangled with that of the inclusive-language NIV (see pp. 183-87); in fact, it was the publication of the NIrV under the title *Kids' Bible* that first alerted Americans to plans for a gender-inclusive NIV. (Those plans were aborted in 1997 but resuscitated in 2002.) The NIrV New Testament was first published in 1994, and the complete Bible in 1996. It was republished in 1998 with a more moderate use of inclusive language. It has been available in Britain since 1998 under the title *New Light Bible*.

The NIrV is aimed at children, adults with reading difficulties and those for whom English is a second language. It has a reading age of 8.6 years, lower even than the ICB, in fact the lowest of any mainline translation. See pages 70-72 for a comparison with the NIV.

THE CONTEMPORARY ENGLISH VERSION (1995)

Alongside the TEV, the CEV is the Bible that most completely incorporates the principles of meaning-driven translation espoused by Eugene Nida. The CEV is a committee translation prepared by the American Bible Society (ABS) and overseen by Barclay Newman.

Like Nida, Newman is experienced as a consultant to missionaries translating the Bible into languages of people-groups that have not previously had the Scriptures and in many cases know little of the gospel. Aware that many English speakers are now almost entirely ignorant of the Bible and even the bare essentials of the Christian faith, Newman's approach to the CEV has been to apply the principles he would use in a missionary context. It is the natural successor to the TEV.

The CEV began life as a collection of Scripture passages relating to the life of Christ, published in a children's illustrated edition in 1986. The warm response encouraged the ABS to proceed with a complete Bible aimed at both children and adults. The New Testament was published in 1991, Psalms and Proverbs the following year, and the complete Bible in 1995.

No translation is more thoroughgoing in its meaning-driven principles than the CEV. Critics say it borders on paraphrase. Table 10.2 offers five New Testament examples that demonstrate how far the CEV diverges from the NIV, a translation that holds to a balance between form-driven and meaning-driven approaches.[5]

The CEV uses everyday, conversational English. Sentences are short, and the vocabulary is simplified. The CEV goes considerably further than the TEV in removing theological language. God's "grace," for instance, becomes God's "kindness," while "parable" becomes "story" and "hosanna" is rendered as "hooray." As one would expect, inclusive language is employed.

Originally intended for children, the CEV has a reading age of 10.3 years (according to the tests on pp. 73-76). The British-spelling edition of the CEV, first published in May 1997, won a Crystal Mark award from the Plain English Campaign. Britain's Scripture Union has adopted the CEV for its Sunday School materials.

The CEV is suitable not only for children but for adults who read very little literature, those for whom English is a second language, and any for whom the Bible is an unexplored book. Two particular features of the CEV are worth highlighting.

Table 10.2. The Meaning-Driven CEV in Comparison to the NIV

Passage	NIV	CEV
Acts 4:33	With great power the apostles continued to testify to the resurrection of the Lord Jesus, and much grace was upon them all.	In a powerful way the apostles told everyone that the Lord Jesus was now alive. God greatly blessed his followers.
Rom 6:1	What shall we say, then? Shall we go on sinning, so that grace may increase?	What should we say? Should we keep on sinning, so that God's wonderful kindness will show up even better?
Gal 1:15-16	But when God, who set me apart from birth and called me by his grace, was pleased to reveal his Son in me so that I might preach him among the Gentiles, I did not consult any man.	But even before I was born, God had chosen me. He was kind and decided to show me his Son, so that I would announce his message to the Gentiles. I didn't talk this over with anyone.
Heb 4:16	Let us then approach the throne of grace with confidence, so that we may receive mercy and find grace to help us in our time of need.	So whenever we are in need, we should come bravely before the throne of our merciful God. There we will be treated with undeserved kindness, and we will find help.
Heb 12:15	See to it that no one misses the grace of God and that no bitter root grows up to cause trouble and defile many.	Make sure that no one misses out on God's wonderful kindness. Don't let anyone become bitter and cause trouble for the rest of you.

The first, at least, is highly praiseworthy. Aware that more people hear the Bible than actually read it for themselves, Newman and his fellow translators took great care over sentence structure and punctuation to ensure that nothing will be misheard. Consider Psalm 109:1-2, as it would be read aloud. The NIV translates the passage as follows:

O God, whom I praise,
do not remain silent,
for wicked and deceitful men

have opened their mouths against me.

The CEV translates it differently:

> I praise you, God!
>> Don't keep silent.
> Destructive and deceitful lies
>> are told about me.

The inexperienced listener to the NIV might easily wonder who the *four* wicked and deceitful men are. But the CEV could be criticized for its tautological "deceitful lies." Try reading Psalm 80:1 aloud from the NIV.

> Hear us, O Shepherd of Israel,
>> you who lead Joseph like a flock;
> you who sit enthroned between the
>> cherubim, shine forth.

The CEV, again, is heard differently.

> Shepherd of Israel, you lead
>> the descendants of Joseph,
> and you sit on your throne
>> above the winged creatures.
> Listen to our prayer
>> and let your light shine.

In the NIV, "you who" in the second and third lines sounds like "yoo hoo"; the passage, when read quickly, could easily stir a giggle from its audience. It is hard to criticize the CEV's translation here, although notice the request that God hear the psalmist has been moved from the first to the third line. It is a shame that more has not been made of the CEV in audio formats.

The other most notable feature of the CEV is its treatment of Old Testament poetry. Much of the figurative language is removed, and in many places the translators have collapsed the Hebrew parallelisms. Table 3.6 (p. 85) explains one example; Job 41:15-17 provides another. The NIV translates the passage thus:

His back has rows of shields
　　tightly sealed together;
each is so close to the next
　　that no air can pass between.
They are joined fast to one another;
　　they cling together and cannot be parted.

The succinctness of the CEV is to be admired.

Its back is covered
　　with shield after shield,
firmly bound and closer together
　　than breath to breath.

Also admirable are the matched phrases "shield after shield" and "breath to breath." However, much has been lost: there is, for example, no equivalent at all for the final sentence in the NIV. It is perhaps partly for this reason, as well as for reasons of accuracy, that in 2003 the ABS announced that a revision of the CEV was in preparation. The fully revised edition was scheduled to release in 2005, just ten years after the original. The ABS has also announced that they wish to have one, global edition of the CEV. At the time of writing it is available in three editions: American, British and with Australasian spellings and idiom.

THE NEW LIVING TRANSLATION (1996; REVISED 2004)

By 1996, twenty-five years after its first appearance as a complete Bible, Kenneth Taylor's LB had sold in excess of forty million copies and was still selling at over half a million a year. The NLT is a thoroughgoing revision of the LB that shifts what was a one-man paraphrase to what is now a genuine team effort, a translation in the meaning-driven mold undertaken over a seven-year period by some ninety American and British scholars. Where Taylor worked from the ASV of 1901, the revisers worked from the original Hebrew and Greek. Taylor's son Mark was one of two English stylists.

　　The NLT claims to be the first adult-level meaning-driven version to be made by evangelical scholars.[6] What the translators of the TEV, NCV or CEV make of that claim is not known, but the NLT can justifiably claim a reading level of eleven years, on a par with the NIV. The NLT is altogether less formal than the NIV, retaining the conversational style of the original LB, but it is not as child-oriented as the TEV or CEV. The revision can be compared to its predecessor in certain verses from John 10:31-42, as shown in table 10.3. A comparison of this and other passages will reveal that not only is the NLT more literal than the LB, it is also more suited to public reading.

Table 10.3. Changes from the LB to the NLT

LB	NLT
[31]Then again the Jewish leaders picked up stones to kill him.	[31]Once again the Jewish leaders picked up stones to kill him. [32]Jesus said, "At my Father's direction I have done many things to help the people. For which one of these good deeds are you killing me?"
[32]Jesus said, "At God's direction I have done many a miracle to help the people. For which one are you killing me?"	
[33]They replied, "Not for any good work, but for blasphemy; you, a mere man, have declared yourself to be God."	[33]They replied, "Not for any good work, but for blasphemy, because you, a mere man, have made yourself God."
[34-36]"In your own Law it says that men are gods!" he replied. "So if the Scripture, which cannot be untrue, speaks of those as gods to whom the message of God came, do you call it blasphemy when one sanctified and sent into the world by the Father says, 'I am the Son of God'?"	[34]Jesus replied, "It is written in your own law that God said to certain leaders of the people, 'I say, you are gods!' [35]And you know that the Scriptures cannot be altered. So if those people, who received God's message, were called 'gods,' [36]why do you call it blasphemy when the Holy One who was sent into the world by the Father says, 'I am the Son of God'? [37]Don't believe me unless I carry out my Father's work. [38]But if I do his work, believe in what I have done, even if you don't believe me. Then you will realize that the Father is in me, and I am in the Father."
[37]"Don't believe me unless I do miracles of God. [38]But if I do, believe them even if you don't believe me. Then you will become convinced that the Father is in me, and I in the Father."	

One professional Bible translator known to me regards the NLT as the best meaning-driven translation available in English and uses it as one of his models for translation into Cheyenne, a native American language. The NLT is well suited to young people and those new to the Christian faith. It is less suited to in-depth study. An anglicized edition of the 1996 NLT was published in 2000; there are as yet no plans to anglicize the 2004 edition.

A deservedly popular study Bible (though more devotional and less academic than, say, the *NIV Study Bible*) that employs the NLT as its basis is the *Life Application Study Bible* (also available in the NIV, AV/KJV, NKJV and NASB). Its publisher, Tyndale House, believes it to be the best-selling study Bible currently on the market.

Since its release, the publishers of the NLT have seen places where precision and style can be further improved, not least in poetic passages. A second edition, with many substantial revisions, was released mid-2004. The amended text will be phased in as current editions need reprinting, including the *Life Application Study Bible* from the the end of 2004.

Isaiah 34:7 provides an example of one proposed change. The NRSV (here identical to the RSV and ESV) is offered by way of a form-driven comparison (see table 10.4). The NRSV does nothing to show that the language is being used figuratively to refer to the slaughter of people, while the NLT removes all figurative references. The NLT second edition retains some figurative elements though at the same time making it clear that the allusion is to violent human death.

Table 10.4. Isaiah 34:7 in Three Versions

NRSV	NLT (1996)	NLT (2004)
Wild oxen shall fall with them, and young steers with the mighty bulls.	The strongest will die—veterans and young men, too.	Even men as strong as wild oxen will die—the young men alongside the veterans.

You may also like to compare John 10:31-38, cited above in the 1996 edition, with its 2004 revision below. Notice how substantial the revisions are and the overall shift taking the translation in a still further form-driven direction:

[31]Once again the people picked up stones to kill him. [32]Jesus said, "At the Father's direction I have done many good works. For which one are you going to stone me?" [33]They replied, "We're

stoning you not for any good work, but for blasphemy! You, a mere man, claim to be God."

[34]Jesus replied, "It is written in your own Scriptures that God said to certain leaders of the people, 'I say, you are gods!' [35]And you know that the Scriptures cannot be altered. So if those people who received God's message were called 'gods,' [36]why do you call it blasphemy when I say, 'I am the Son of God'? After all, the Father set me apart and sent me into the world. [37]Don't believe me unless I carry out my Father's work. [38]But if I do his work, believe in the evidence of the miraculous works I have done, even if you don't believe me. Then you will know and understand that the Father is in me, and I am in the Father."

The NLT second edition is one of several translations to appear so far in the twenty-first century. Its text is now available within the iLumina software program. Additionally, a new study Bible based on the second edition is expected in 2006 or 2007. Other twenty-first-century versions are the subject of the next chapter.

INTO A NEW MILLENNIUM

*The Word became flesh and blood, and
moved into the neighborhood.*

JOHN 1:14 *THE MESSAGE*

𝒢

As the twentieth century turned into the twenty-first, the two most notable features of the English Bible translation scene were the increasing polarization between form-driven and meaning-driven translations, and the continuing debate over gender-inclusive language. *The Message* by Eugene Peterson illustrates the first; development of the NIV exemplifies the second.

THE MESSAGE (1993-2002)

Eugene Peterson's unique paraphrase of the New Testament made an immediate and deep impact when first published in 1993. Since then, section by section, portions of the Old Testament have appeared at regular intervals: the Psalms in 1994; Proverbs in 1995; the Wisdom books in 1998; the Prophets in 2000; the Pentateuch in 2001; and the Historical Books, together with the complete Bible, in July 2002. The complete Bible shows some signs of revision: for example, in the Psalms "Yahweh" now becomes "GOD."

The Message is a paraphrase that people either love or loathe. Previous examples of the genre, such as the LB or the work of J. B. Phillips, look tame by comparison. The genius of *The Message* lies in Peterson's abilities as a wordsmith. He writes with passion and power, almost turning prose into poetry. He composes with an elevated style, often staccato in effect, and also has a liking for hyphenated word-strings. An example of these features is found in John 1:14:

> The Word became flesh and blood,
>> and moved into the neighborhood.
> We saw the glory with our own eyes,
>> the one-of-a-kind glory,
>> like Father, like Son,
> Generous inside and out,
>> true from start to finish.

On occasions, a little too much liberty is taken with the text, and there are some anachronisms that make the intelligent reader look twice. In Genesis 28:19, after Jacob dreamed of a stairway to the sky, did he actually "christen" the place Bethel? Naturally, all the usual warnings about the dangers of paraphrases being interpretive must also be sounded. *The Message* should not replace a more reliable translation, but it is a valuable tool in refreshing one's interest in Bible reading or in glimpsing something of the impact it must have made on its first readers.

THE NIV GOES INCLUSIVE (1997)

In late 1996, it became known that the International Bible Society (IBS) and the NIV's Committee for Bible Translation (CBT) were planning the publication of an inclusive-language or "gender-neutral" NIV. Opposition to the NIVi was swift and heated. Matters were not helped by a statement in the preface to the proposed NIVi: "It is often appropriate to mute the patriarchalism of the culture of the biblical writers through gender-inclusive language." This suggested to some that the CBT wanted not merely to respond to changes in the English language but to rewrite Bible history, something that was never their intention.

Opposition was spearheaded by two organizations: Focus on the Family, whose president, James Dobson, is an American household name; and the Council on Biblical Manhood and Womanhood, then presided over by theologian Wayne Grudem. The powerful and theologically conservative Southern Baptist Convention later also denounced the NIVi.

The debate was further inflamed by reporting in some parts of the Christian press. *World* magazine earned a public rebuke from the Evangelical Press Association for describing the NIVi as a "stealth Bible" employing "unisex language" with an agenda of "feminist seduction." Many more magazine and newspaper articles followed; there were even some lengthy debates on radio.

On May 27, 1997, at a meeting called by Dobson, the IBS announced its decision to halt publication of the NIVi and to revise the recently published gender-inclusive NIrV for children (see p. 174 for more details). The IBS also stated that "the present (1984) NIV text will continue to be published" and that "there are no plans for a further revised edition."[1] Five years later, the IBS announced publication of Today's New International Version (see pp. 186-87), complete with "gender-accurate" language. Some regarded the announcement as a breach of the undertaking made in 1997. Others would say the original commitment was made under undue pressure. Nevertheless, the IBS is honoring its commitment to keep the standard NIV in print as long as there is a demand for it.

Although the NIVi never saw the light of day in North America, publication had already gone ahead in Britain. The New Testament appeared in November 1996, and the complete Bible in April 1997, just six weeks before publication was halted in the United States. British publishers Hodder & Stoughton declined a request from IBS to withdraw the anglicized NIVi, contracts already having been signed and copies sold. Hodder & Stoughton did, however, make a money-back offer to anyone buying an NIVi from them who did not like the inclusive language.

The NIVi never stirred up the controversy in Britain that it provoked in North America. In fact, the Christian public in Britain was largely apathetic; those who did know what was taking place across the Atlantic were bemused and bewildered by the fuss. Young readers, readers with strong opinions about political correctness, or those simply wanting to keep up to date did purchase the NIVi. Others decided to stick with the Bible they knew. Ministers who adopted the NIVi had to answer questions from members of the congregation who had a different version in their pews and at home.

The CBT has admitted that the introduction of inclusive language to the NIV was undertaken in too wholesale a manner and, in places, quite carelessly. Table 11.1 shows Mark 8:34-38 in the NIV, the NIVi and the later TNIV. A few points are worthy of note:

- The NIVi can be clumsy, especially in verse 38: "the Son of Man will be ashamed of when . . ."

- The TNIV uses *their* as a *singular* pronoun in verses 34 and 35.

- The TNIV continues the second-person from verse 36 to verse 38; the NIVi reverts to the third-person plural in verse 38.

- Neither the NIVi nor the TNIV attempt to change Jesus' title "Son of Man."

Table 11.1. Gender Treatment in the NIV Family

NIV (1984)	NIVi (1997)	TNIV (NT 2002)
[34]Then he called the crowd to him along with his disciples and said: "If anyone would come after me, he must deny himself and take up his cross and follow me. [35]For whoever wants to save his life will lose it, but whoever loses his life for me and for the gospel will save it. [36]What good is it for a man to gain the whole world, yet forfeit his soul? [37]Or what can a man give in exchange for his soul? [38]If anyone is ashamed of me and my words in this adulterous and sinful generation, the Son of Man will be ashamed of him when he comes in his Father's glory with the holy angels."	[34]Then he called the crowd to him along with his disciples and said: "Those who would come after me must deny themselves and take up their cross and follow me. [35]For those who want to save their lives will lose them, but those who lose their lives for me and for the gospel will save them. [36]What good is it for you to gain the whole world, yet forfeit your soul? [37]Or what can you give in exchange for your soul? [38]All who are ashamed of me and my words in this adulterous and sinful generation, the Son of Man will be ashamed of when he comes in his Father's glory with the holy angels."	[34]Then he called the crowd to him along with his disciples and said: "Those who would be my disciples must deny themselves and take up their cross and follow me. [35]For those who want to save their life will lose it, but those who lose their life for me and for the gospel will save it. [36]What good is it for you to gain the whole world, yet forfeit your soul? [37]Or what can you give in exchange for your soul? [38]If any of you are ashamed of me and my words in this adulterous and sinful generation, the Son of Man will be ashamed of you when he comes in his Father's glory with the holy angels."

TODAY'S NEW INTERNATIONAL VERSION (2005)

Zondervan put the "gender-accurate" TNIV New Testament on sale in March 2002. A British edition was published unobtrusively the following month by Hodder & Stoughton. In the United States all the previous arguments were revisited, in newspaper articles, in radio interviews and on the Internet. This time the IBS was better prepared and marshalled its arguments carefully.

The TNIV represents more than just a second attempt at introducing inclusive language to the NIV. Approximately 7 percent of the text has been changed, and two-thirds of these changes are entirely unrelated to gender. There are many small alterations that make the TNIV more precise and generally crisper than the NIV. Some of these remove remaining archaisms; for example, Mary is said to be "pregnant" rather than "with child"; the "sixth hour" becomes "noon"; and the vocative "O" (as in "O Lord") is omitted. Others relate to advances in scholarship and the understanding of technical expressions. So, for instance, the "basic principles" of the world become "elemental spiritual forces" (Col 2:8). "Christ" often becomes "Messiah" where this functions as a title; "saints" often becomes "people of God"; and "the Jews" becomes "Jewish leaders" where this is the sense (see pp. 98-100 for more on this point). There are also minor changes in paragraph and sentence structure, word order, spelling, punctuation, and the placement and wording of some section headings. One survey suggests that of all the changes made, other than those relating to gender, three out of four move the TNIV toward "a more essentially literal rendering" in comparison with the NIV.[2]

As to inclusive language, the TNIV incorporates this in a stylistically less heavy-handed manner than did the NIVi. The TNIV was carefully billed as being "gender-accurate" rather than gender-inclusive. Interestingly, the TNIV does use one device not so consistently found in the earlier NIVi, namely singular *they*, *them* and *their*. An example of this is found in Luke 17:3. Here, in the standard NIV, Jesus says to his disciples, "If your brother sins, rebuke him, and if he repents, forgive him." The TNIV has, "If any brother or sister sins against you, rebuke the offender, and if *they* repent, forgive *them*." In this particular sentence, "they" and "them" refer to one brother or one sister.

Some grammatical purists argue that *they* and *them* should be used only to indicate the plural. However, singular *they* is commonly used in everyday speech where the speaker does not know or does not want to reveal an individual's gender. For instance, "My daughter's friend came yesterday, but *they* only stayed an hour." But how appropriate singular *they* is in formal writing will always be a matter of debate.[3]

In places, when compared to the NIV, the TNIV seems to move slightly in the direction of a form-driven philosophy: the translation is often tighter. But elsewhere it moves in a meaning-driven direction. For example, John 1:18, which in the NIV speaks of "God the One and Only, who is at the Father's side," becomes "the one and only Son, who is himself God and is in closest relationship with the Father."

At the time of writing, only the TNIV New Testament is available, and the controversy surrounding it is ongoing. Until the complete Bible is ready, it is not possible to say how popular it will prove to be. A grave danger is that inclusive language will be a point of division or even become a test of orthodoxy. Arguably, the NIV, as the most widely used and accepted modern version, had the potential to become the new "authorized" version, bringing Christians (at least Protestant ones) together around one common text. This potential is now severely damaged. Two translations, discussed below, were born in part out of opposition to an inclusive-language NIV.

THE ENGLISH STANDARD VERSION (2001)

Opponents of the inclusive NIV met in Colorado Springs to draw up more conservative guidelines for the rendering of passages with a generic meaning. At the same time, they also began to discuss the merits of updating the RSV (1952). Where proponents of an evangelical revision of the RSV had failed in the 1960s, Wayne Grudem succeeded in September 1998. With sales of the RSV now relatively low (the replacement NRSV having been published in 1990), the National Council of Churches of Christ, copyright holders of the RSV, saw no objection in granting permission for revision.

Under the chief editorship of Professor Jim Packer of Regent College, a fourteen-member oversight committee was supplemented by a translation review board of some fifty scholars working on individual Bible books, and a further fifty on an advisory council, whose main purpose seems to have been to endorse the translation. People from both North America and Britain appear on all three panels.

The ESV was published by Crossway Books in October 2001, selling 80,000 copies in the first four months. A British edition followed in April 2002 under the Collins imprint. All standard editions include 76,000 center-column cross-references and a 14,500-entry concordance. Where the RSV had running heads, the ESV employs section headings. American editions have maps and book introductions, and come with a free electronic version on CD-ROM. A study Bible is planned for a future, as of yet unspecified date.

The ESV is best described as a light revision of the RSV. Apart from the removal of archaic "thee/thou" terminology, which the RSV retained in relation to God, and a policy of moderate, if formulaic, inclusive language (following the Colorado Springs guidelines), no more than 3-4 percent of the RSV text has been updated.

Given its background, the ESV is more gender-inclusive than one might expect. However, unlike the NRSV and other gender-inclusive Bibles, it never turns a third-person singular into a plural in order to disguise male-oriented language. The rather formulaic approach to gender issues has created some oddities: for instance, in John 2:24-25, "all people" is followed by "man": "But Jesus on his part did not entrust himself to them, because he knew all people [25]and needed no one to bear witness about man, for he himself knew what was in man."

Similarly, in Ephesians 4:13, the ESV states that the goal of ministry is a "mature manhood," but a few verses later Paul calls upon his readers to "put off your old self" (RSV "old man"). Following the Colorado Springs guidelines, "manhood" translates *anēr*, while the old or new "self" translates *anthrōpos* (see pp. 94-95 for more on this point).

The ESV introduces other revisions to the RSV for one of three reasons: for greater literalness; for closer concordance (employing, where possible, the same English word for all occurrences of a particular Hebrew or Greek word); or to use more up-to-date vocabulary (e.g., "troughs" for the RSV's "runnels" in Gen 30:38, 41, and "jug of oil" for "cruse of oil" in 1 Kings 17:12-16). Regrettably, not all of the advances in scholarship incorporated in the NRSV have found their way into the theologically more conservative ESV.

In style, the ESV remains closer to the RSV than does the NRSV. Only rarely is the ESV more idiomatic than the RSV. Certainly, the ESV has more "Bible English" in places where the NRSV has a more natural style. Hence, some reviewers have found the ESV a little awkward in places such as Mark 8:34, with its jarring word order: "And he called to him the crowd." Another example, where again the ESV makes no alteration to the structure order of the RSV, is Isaiah 22:17: "Behold, the LORD will . . . seize firm hold on you." But generally the ESV reads well and justifiably claims to be well suited to public reading, liturgical use and memorization.

The ESV "corrects" a number of verses to which, in the RSV, conservative evangelicals had taken exception half a century previously (see table 11.2).

Table 11.2. ESV "Corrections" to the RSV

Passage	RSV (1971 edition)	ESV	Notes
Is 7:14	young woman	virgin	Cf. Mt 1:23
Gen 22:17-18, etc.	descendants (pl.)	offspring (sing.)	Cf. Gal 3:16
Ps 2:7	my son	my Son	—
Ps 2:11-12	kiss his feet	kiss the Son	—
Ps 45:6	your divine throne	your throne, O God	—
Rom 1:17	He who through faith is righteous shall live.	The righteous shall live by faith.	Cf. Hab 2:4
Rom 3:25, etc.	expiation	propitiation	—
Rom 9:5	Christ who is God over all	Christ. God who is over all	Cf. Mt 1:23

In the Old Testament, the ESV adheres rigidly to the Masoretic Text, accepting variant readings only rarely—far less often than the RSV, the NRSV or even the NIV, though more often than the NASB. In regard to Old Testament messianic references, however, the ESV is not as conservative as the NIV. In a number of Old Testament passages, the NIV draws attention to their messianic interpretation by the use of capitals, where the ESV does not (see p. 87). Table 11.3 lists some of these.

Table 11.3. Capitalization in the ESV and the NIV

Passage	ESV	NIV
Ps 2:2	his anointed	his Anointed One
Ps 16:10	holy one	Holy One
Dan 9:26	anointed one	Anointed One

The ESV will appeal to those who want a trustworthy and accurate translation, free from interpretive renderings and transparent to the style of the original text. It will be appreciated as well by those who formerly used the RSV or who want a Bible that clearly stands within the Tyndale/KJV tradition but is free from archaisms. But not all will be convinced that its biblical scholarship is as up to date as it could be or its style as natural as might have been achieved even without compromise to its form-driven principles.

Table 11.4 demonstrates how the ESV's English is sometimes more conservative and less natural than that of the NRSV, often leaving the RSV unchanged. The list includes all the verses highlighted on pp. 170-71, together with a few more.

It is also helpful to compare a complete passage in all three versions. Romans 3:21-26 is given in table 11.5. The NASB's and CEV's renderings of the same verses are found on p. 35.

Table 11.4. Changes to the RSV in the ESV and NRSV

Passage	RSV	ESV	NRSV
Gen 1:1	In the beginning God created . . .	As RSV	In the beginning when God created . . .
Gen 1:6	firmament	expanse	dome
Deut 29:5	Your sandals have not worn off your feet.	As RSV	The sandals on your feet have not worn out.
Ps 39:9	I am dumb	I am mute	I am silent
Amos 6:5	. . . like David invent for themselves instruments of music	As RSV	. . . like David improvise on instruments of music
Zech 3:3	Now Joshua was standing before the angel, clothed in filthy garments.	As RSV	Now Joshua was dressed with filthy clothes as he stood before the angel.
Mt 1:18	betrothed	As RSV	engaged
Lk 22:35	"Did you lack anything?" They said, "Nothing."	As RSV	"Did you lack anything?" They said, "No, not a thing."
2 Cor 11:25	Once I was stoned.	As RSV	Once I received a stoning.
Eph 3:16	. . . grant you to be strengthened with might by his Spirit in the inner man	. . . grant you to be strengthened with power through his Spirit in your inner being	. . . grant that you may be strengthened in your inner being with power through his Spirit
Rev 2:29	He who has an ear, let him hear what the Spirit says to the churches.	As RSV	Let anyone who has an ear listen to what the Spirit is saying to the churches.

Table 11.5. Romans 3:21-26 in the RSV and Its Revisions

RSV (1971 revision)	ESV (2001)	NRSV (1990)
[21]But now the righteousness of God has been manifested apart from law, although the law and the prophets bear witness to it, [22]the righteousness of God through faith in Jesus Christ for all who believe. For there is no distinction; [23]since all have sinned and fall short of the glory of God, [24]they are justified by his grace as a gift, through the redemption which is in Christ Jesus, [25]whom God put forward as an expiation by his blood, to be received by faith. This was to show God's righteousness, because in his divine forbearance he had passed over former sins; [26]it was to prove at the present time that he himself is righteous and that he justifies him who has faith in Jesus.	[21]But now the righteousness of God has been manifested apart from the law, although the Law and the Prophets bear witness to it— [22]the righteousness of God through faith in Jesus Christ for all who believe. For there is no distinction: [23]for all have sinned and fall short of the glory of God, [24]and are justified by his grace as a gift, through the redemption that is in Christ Jesus, [25]whom God put forward as a propitiation by his blood, to be received by faith. This was to show God's righteousness, because in his divine forbearance he had passed over former sins. [26]It was to show his righteousness at the present time, so that he might be just and the justifier of the one who has faith in Jesus.	[21]But now, apart from law, the righteousness of God has been disclosed, and is attested by the law and the prophets, [22]the righteousness of God through faith in Jesus Christ for all who believe. For there is no distinction, [23]since all have sinned and fall short of the glory of God; [24]they are now justified by his grace as a gift, through the redemption that is in Christ Jesus, [25]whom God put forward as a sacrifice of atonement by his blood, effective through faith. He did this to show his righteousness, because in his divine forbearance he had passed over the sins previously committed; [26]it was to prove at the present time that he himself is righteous and that he justifies the one who has faith in Jesus.

This look at the ESV completes the revisions of the Bible that stand in the Tyndale/KJV tradition. Figure 11.1 summarizes the history.

THE HOLMAN CHRISTIAN STANDARD BIBLE (2004)

The HCSB is the product of the Southern Baptist Convention (SBC) and, like the ESV, was conceived as an alternative to the inclusive-language NIVi. The SBC Sunday School Board, which previously used the NIV for all its materials, found itself concerned with the NIV on two counts: the controversy surrounding the introduction of inclusive lan-

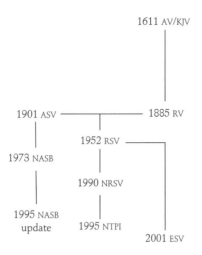

Figure 11.1. Bible versions in the Tyndale/KJV tradition

guage, against which SBC Secretary Paige Patterson spoke out very vigorously; and the high cost of using the NIV under license.

In 1998, the SBC Sunday School Board entered into an agreement with Art Farstad (the man behind the NKJV) to complete the production of a new version on which he had commenced work in 1984. Although Farstad died in 1998, the $10 million project continued under the editorship of Ed Blum, a former professor at Dallas Theological College and Farstad's assistant. One major change was the adoption of the latest Greek texts: Farstad had employed the Greek underlying the AV/KJV, as he had for the NKJV. In all, a team of nearly eighty scholars worked on the HCSB. The translation takes its name from Broadman and Holman, the publishing agency for the SBC.

As a translation, the HCSB is more literal than the NIV but less literal than the NASB or ESV. It has a fair amount of Bible English and shows clear signs of being influenced by the Tyndale/KJV tradition, but it cannot be said to stand within that tradition. Its motto is "precision with clarity," and its goal is "optimal equivalence." The latter phrase appears to mean that while the translators have given priority to a form-driven approach, they have been prepared to use moderate meaning-driven methods when necessary for the sake of creating readable English. Where a meaning-driven rendering appears in the text, a more literal translation is offered in the footnotes. Pronouns are capitalized when referring to God, Jesus Christ or the Holy Spirit.

On gender issues the HCSB follows the same Colorado Springs guidelines drawn up in 1997 and adhered to by the ESV. Hence, there are some concessions to inclusive language (e.g., "men" regularly becomes "people"), but masculine pronouns *he, his* and *him* are retained, where other translations such as the NRSV and TNIV prefer to pluralize a sentence.

The HCSB Gospels appeared in 1999, the New Testament in June 2001, and the Psalms and Proverbs in 2003. The complete Bible came online at <http://bible.lifeway.com> in late 2003 and was published in print form in April 2004. Its Southern Baptist backing is certain to guarantee it a high level of support in the United States, though predominantly from conservative evangelical churches. With its clear style, excellent footnotes and cross-references, it promises to be a useful Bible for study purposes; its slight woodenness may limit its public use.

BIBLES ON THE INTERNET

It will come as little surprise to discover that the peculiar properties of the Internet are being employed in promoting English Bible translations. Not only are most translations now readily available on the Internet, but it is also being used in the tasks of translation, publication and dissemination. Before the advent of electronic communication, most cooperative translation work was undertaken by scholars meeting in committee once, twice or several times a year to review and edit their individual work. This was the approach of the AV/KJV, RSV, NIV and NRSV. But because the Internet permits high-speed viewing and transmission of easily editable text, the whole process can be radically altered. For example:

- Translators can confer with one another almost instantaneously. They can send each other portions of text, repeatedly editing them with ease.

- A large number of people, both expert and lay, can comment on a translation, even before it has reached its final form. Corrections can be made at any stage.
- Even after "completion," revisions can be made on a continual basis. There is no need to wait for ten or twenty years for a new edition.
- Online readers can view and download the latest edition of the text at any time.
- The text can be distributed on CD-ROM and incorporated into Bible software programs allowing powerful search and cross-reference facilities.

Three Bible translations, all developed and distributed on the Internet, are worthy of mention.

The NET Bible. The NET (New English Translation) Bible is a continually evolving version. Its home is <www.bible.org/netbible>.[4] It is available online, on CD-ROM or as downloadable software for Windows or Macintosh computers, in Palm-compatible and Pocket PC formats, as MP3 audio files and (if you really want it) as a book. Work is still proceeding on the Apocrypha.

The most obvious and noticeable feature of the NET Bible is its large number of footnotes—60,237 in the 2003 second beta edition. As a translation, there is little that is remarkable about the NET's rendering of the biblical text: the uneven translation varies from moderately form-driven to moderately meaning-driven. But its wealth of notes turns it into a technical study Bible for those who want a shortcut to the Hebrew and Greek without actually having to learn either language.

The NET Bible offers three levels of notes: text critical notes dealing with variant readings of the underlying Hebrew or Greek; translation notes explaining the rationale behind a particular rendering and possible alternative translations; and study notes encompassing a wider discussion of a text's background and interpretation. The printed edition and some software editions also contain some wonderful satellite-generated maps, cross-references to which are footnoted in the text.

Anyone can submit a question, suggest an alteration or challenge the translation of a particular verse in the NET Bible. Valid comments are taken up into the translation or its notes. The NET Bible is proving to be a valuable tool for missionaries undertaking Bible translation work.

The WEB. The WEB (World English Bible), unlike the NET Bible and the ISV (below), is not an original translation but a revision of the 1901 ASV. For the most part, early stages of the revision (e.g., updating archaic language) were done automatically by computer. The later stages are being done manually.

The WEB is largely the work of one person, Michael Paul Johnson, who, interestingly, does not claim to know Hebrew or Greek but seems to rely on consulting various scholarly tomes. He invites others to comment on his revision and to suggest changes. Being a revision of the ASV, the WEB definitely falls into the form-driven category.

A welcome feature of the WEB is that no attempt has been made to copyright it. It is freely available in the public domain and can be copied electronically or in printed form without restriction. It can be downloaded in a variety of formats. As of 2003, a printed version of the New Testament, Psalms and Proverbs was available. Work continues on the Old Testament. The relevant website is <http://ebible.org/bible/web>. Further information can also be found on <www.worldenglishbible.com>.

The International Standard Version. The ISV is a moderately form-driven translation with a good English style. It contains relatively little Bible English. Except in its distinctive poetry (see below), it is perhaps just slightly more literal than the NIV. Some sensitivity is shown toward gender issues, but it is not a thoroughgoing gender-inclusive version like the NRSV, for example. The ISV is an entirely new translation, not a revision. Some of the core translation team are Christians with a Jewish background.

To date, only the New Testament and about a third of the Old have been completed. These are available on the translator's website: <http://isv.org>. A printed New Testament with Psalms and Proverbs is also available. Both printed and downloadable versions include section headings, parallel passages, cross-references and footnotes.

The ISV has two distinctive features: it attempts to express the nuances of NT Greek tenses; and more noticeably, it sets out poetry in metrical rhyme. An example of the latter is taken from 2 Timothy 2:11-13:

In dying with Christ, true life we gain.
Enduring, we with him shall reign.
Who him denies, he will disclaim.
Our faith may fail, his never wanes—
For thus he is, he cannot change!

Having made the journey from the songs of Caedmon to the high-speed age of the Internet, it is now time to make some reflections and perhaps draw some conclusions—the task of the final chapter.

12

REFLECTIONS
AND CONCLUSIONS

Take the veil from my eyes,

that I may see the wonders to be found in your law.

PSALM 119:18 REB

࿔

In concluding this overview of translation principles (part one of the book) and actual translations (part two), I want to draw two kinds of conclusion: first, from the wider and more general perspective of English Bible translations; and second, from the personal perspective of choosing a Bible.

THE WIDER PICTURE

The reader will have picked up from this book many of the trends that are current in English Bible translation. We should applaud the sheer quality of English Bible translations. Never at any point in history has any language been as well served by the general accuracy and stylistic range of first-rate translations that are available. Apart from those who first read the Scriptures in their original languages, no generation has ever been closer to God's Word.

If, however, the quality is to be praised, the sheer quantity must give rise to concern. The human and financial resources that go into a committee-organized translation are near incalculable: tens of thousands of translation hours and tens of millions of dollars (in recent years only U.S. groups have been able to fund such large projects). One cannot help wondering: would world mission be better served if more of these resources were diverted into translating the Bible into languages that do not yet have even their first Bible translation?

Regrettably, the recent story of English Bible translation has been one of competition as much as it has been one of cooperation. Vested theological and financial interests do not serve either the church or the cause of mission well. The continuing and deepening distrust between those who use and promote translations from different theological backgrounds—evangelical, ecumenical and Roman Catholic—means that a universal acceptance of one version for all English-speaking Christians remains a dream. For three and a half centuries the AV/KJV stood as a monument to Christian unity—or, at least, unity among Protestants. The translators of the RSV hoped to carry that dream further by creating a Bible acceptable to all English-speaking Christians, but its failure to win the support of the powerful conservative evangelical lobby, and the creation of the NIV as an evangelical alternative, left that dream shattered.

Today, the rift has reappeared in a new guise. Where once it was over *expiation* versus *propitiation* and *young woman* versus *virgin*, it is now fought over *brother* versus *brother and sister* and *men* versus *people*. The inclusive-language debate has been fueled not only by legitimate linguistic issues but by partisan theological motives. That the choice of a Bible version or particular features of a translation should be a test of orthodoxy is a shameful scandal that only damages the witness of the Christian church.

The last forty years have also seen an increasing divergence in translation philosophy. The debate continues over form-driven versus meaning-driven translations. For a few years it swings one way, then the other. Currently, the debate is more polarized than ever before, leaving the Christian public confused. Whereas once the issue was seen as purely linguistic, it is now seen as theological. New translations are likely to be at one end of the spectrum or the other. Middle-ground translations are losing out. Because of its dominant market share and evangelical sensitivities, the NIV has proved to be the most fought-over battleground, just as it has been in the inclusive-language debate.

The truth, however, is that we need both form-driven and meaning-driven translations. Wise Christians will equip themselves with at least one of each and compare them regularly. The greatest danger of inaccuracy and the misrepresentation of God's Word lies in the extremes, whether it be in the direction of excessively form-driven or excessively meaning-driven versions. What are needed are translations in the middle range between reasonably form-driven and moderately meaning-driven. Translations outside this range—ultraliteral renderings on the one hand and paraphrases on the other—have their place, but not as a Christian's standard Bible.

With the arrival of ever more translations and revisions, the short-lived nature of some versions must be counted as a further worry. Revisions of some Bibles, notably those in the meaning-driven camp, are being planned almost before the ink is dry on the first version. The NLT and CEV are two examples, both undergoing revision after less than ten years in print. And the onset of online Bibles that can be updated continuously is a factor militating against a much-needed personal familiarity with Scripture: the laudable practice of verse memorization has all but ceased.

Beyond these areas of concern, there are some more welcome trends. One is the increasing recognition of the need for Bibles that sound right when being read aloud, particularly in the context of public worship. Today, more people hear God's Word than read it for themselves. A recognition of this need for clarity and euphony is found in both form-driven and meaning-driven translations, the NRSV and CEV being good examples respectively.

A further welcome trend is the growing availability of online and electronic Bibles. In some cases, this simply means that an existing print-based Bible is available in a computer-based format; in other cases, it has come to mean whole new translations such as the NET Bible.

While the added number of translations and the possibility of constant revision is a downside, the powerful search and study software in the CD-ROM packages that accompany many electronic Bibles is a definite plus-point. Any number of translations can be compared side by side on a computer screen, or a favorite translation can be downloaded into an easily pocketable handheld device several times smaller than any printed Bible.

All of the above must be set against the decline of biblical literacy in the population at large and even among churchgoing Christians. The rise of so many alternatives (including TV, video and computer) to the printed book as a source of information or entertainment is a major contributing factor, but the sheer number of Bible translations in a near limitless number of editions cannot be overlooked.

Understandably, Christian publishing agencies have felt a need to respond to the decline in Bible reading. But whether saturating the market with such a glut of Bibles is part of the answer or part of the problem is highly debatable. Making the Bible ever easier to read (through meaning-driven translations with lower reading levels), and making it ever easier to understand (with more and more annotated versions and study Bibles) is just as likely to devalue God's Word as it is to inspire people toward reading and studying it for themselves. There is real danger in dumbing down the Scriptures. Bringing something down to our level does not necessarily lift us up to its level.

At the time of this writing, translations and revisions known to be in the pipeline (along with their anticipated release dates) include

- CEV revision (2004 or beyond)
- ISV (awaiting two thirds of OT)
- NET Bible (awaiting Apocrypha; the rest under constant revision)
- TNIV (awaiting OT in the fall of 2005)

THE PERSONAL PERSPECTIVE

This book began with two questions: Why so many translations? And which of these is best? I hope that the first question has been answered, but only the reader can answer the second. It boils down to two questions: Best for whom? And best for what? A Bible that suits a mature Christian may not be easily understood by a new believer. One prepared for adults may not be suitable for children. One that is appreciated by a university-educated person is not usually right for someone whose education finished at sixteen.

Similarly, the translation that is suited to personal study may not be the best for reading aloud or for liturgical use. And the one that is good for devotional reading may not be ideal for group study. But knowing the range of Bibles available and understanding the translation philosophy underlining them will help in making an informed choice. And even when the question "Which translation?" has been resolved, there are issues surrounding "Which edition?" (See the discussion in chapter five.) For instance, do I want a study Bible? One with or without the Apocrypha? One with or without cross-references or a concordance?

But remaining solely with the question of "Which translation?" I will stick my neck out a little further and suggest some guiding principles.

There is little point, except for nostalgic reasons, in choosing an older translation over its revision. Revisions nearly always improve upon their predecessors and are invariably more accurate. It would make sense, therefore, to choose the NLT over the LB, the NJB over the JB, the REB over the NEB, the NRSV or ESV over the RSV, the NASBu over the NASB and, if inclusive language is acceptable to you, the TNIV over the NIV.

An exception to this rule must be the AV/KJV. Although we now have revisions of revisions of revisions of the AV/KJV, and despite its obvious drawbacks, the Bible of 1611 has a unique place in the history of English translations. It cannot be recommended for study purposes, or for its reliability of text or translation, but neither can it be surpassed for literary quality. For giving us the AV/KJV and for influencing so many later revisions, the name of William Tyndale must be held in the highest honor.

Among modern versions—those from the mid-1970s to the present—I hesitate to make specific recommendations. Most Christians have one preferred translation, and anything that strengthens familiarity with it is to be encouraged. But from time to time it is worth considering a change. Revisions and new translations that offer significant improvements regularly become available. If you do not want to make a complete change, then at least think about regularly consulting a second translation alongside your preferred version.

It is particularly useful to have a form-driven version alongside one that is meaning-driven. Comparing a word-for-word version with a meaning-for-meaning one is always enlightening and instructive. Among major Protestant translations, one might choose the NASB, NRSV or ESV alongside the NLT, TEV or CEV (see tables 2.6 and 3.6 for a more complete comparative list).

The NIV is rightly popular as a middle-of-the-road translation. Many evangelical Christians never read anything else. But while the NIV is an excellent multipurpose Bible, it is still worthwhile to complement it with a translation that is either more literal or more free, for instance, the NRSV or the ESV on the one hand or the NLT on the other. In a group Bible-study setting, it can be very helpful if two or three translations are available, representing different translation approaches. For either personal or group use, a paraphrase such as *The Message* can be great to dip into but should never be used as a principal Bible.

For children, the CEV, TEV, NIrV and ICB can all be recommended. Of these four, only the ICB is specifically a children's Bible, while the NIrV does upgrade the standard NIV. For teenagers, look for special editions of the NCV.

Choosing a version for church use and public reading is harder, as it is impractical to have more than one pew Bible. Consideration should be given to two main factors: Which translation will suit a particular church's style of worship, and which will read well? For some churches, a third factor will be inclusive language. The following would make a good shortlist: NRSV, (T)NIV, ESV and REB.

The preface to any translation will indicate the translation philosophy and textual choices underlying the particular version. It will also tell the reader how to interpret any abbreviations used in the footnotes and how to get the best from any special features such as cross-references. As such, reading the preface is highly recommended.

Once, an advertisement for a particular translation (it need not be named) showed several Bibles, each in a different color. The caption read "You can have any *color* you like, so long as it is *read* all over." Amen to that. Survey after survey reveals the sad fact that the Bible is being read and studied in private by fewer and fewer churchgoing Christians. And among unbelievers, a high percentage have never in their lives opened a copy. Has the plethora of translations added to the problem or will it help solve the problem? It is hard to tell. All the arguments in the world about the merits and demerits of this translation or that version matter not one bit unless we are regularly feeding, alone and with others, on the precious Word of Life—and then applying it to our lives.

> Blessed Lord,
> who caused all holy Scriptures to be written for our learning:
> help us so to hear them,
> to read, mark, learn, and inwardly digest them
> that, through patience, and the comfort of your holy word,
> we may embrace and for ever hold fast the hope of
>   everlasting life,
> which you have given us in our Saviour Jesus Christ.[1]

APPENDIX 1

BEING ORIGINAL

Not one original biblical manuscript exists—or if any do, they have yet to be dug up. All we have are copies, in most cases several times removed from the original: copies of copies of copies. Some are in the original languages: Hebrew for the Old Testament, Greek for the New Testament; some are translations into other languages such as Latin.

Before translators can begin their task, they must make a decision about the underlying text from which they will be working. Many thousands of biblical manuscripts exist: significant variations between them are marked in the footnotes that appear in most Bibles. How have these manuscripts come down to us (a process known as *transmission*), and how do translators decide which is most likely to preserve the now lost original (a process called *textual criticism*)?

TRANSMISSION: THE OLD TESTAMENT

The process of transmission is very different depending on whether one is looking at the Old or the New Testament. I begin by looking at the Old Testament.

Masoretic Text. The standard Hebrew Bible from which Old Testament translators work contains the Masoretic Text (MT). By the second century A.D., the Hebrew Bible had been standardized by Jewish scholars. Prior to this, some books circulated with considerable variation in their text. The book of Jeremiah, for example, is known to have existed in two editions, one nearly 20 percent longer than the other. In c. A.D. 112 a Jewish council—the Synod of Jamnia—confirmed what, over the preceding century, Jews had come to accept as the settled biblical text.

Once standardized, considerable care was taken in the copying of this text. Between c. A.D. 500 and c. 1100, the task of preserving and transmitting the text was undertaken by scholars called Masoretes (after *māsôrâ*, meaning "handed down"). It was the Masoretes who added the vowel marks found in modern editions of the Hebrew Bible. Prior to that, biblical Hebrew was written without vowels, but as it fell into disuse as a living language, help was needed in the pronunciation of the text.

The greatest of the Masorete scholars were from the ben Asher family. For five or six generations they faithfully copied the biblical text, perfecting a system of vowel points, accents and marginal notations. They copied the text accurately even when it was obvious that it contained mistakes, putting what they considered the correct reading in the margin. The oldest surviving Masoretic manuscript is *Codex Aleppo*, so called because it was kept for centuries by a Jewish congregation in Aleppo, Syria (*codex* refers to a book as opposed to a scroll). It was the work of Aaron ben Asher, the last of the ben Asher family, and can be dated to c. A.D. 925. It once contained the entire Hebrew Bible, but sadly the opening books were destroyed by fire. The remaining books are now in Jerusalem.

Apart from *Codex Aleppo*, there are several other copies of the MT in existence that date from the tenth and eleventh centuries. One of the few that is complete is *Codex Leningrad*. This dates to A.D. 1008 and is a direct copy of a manuscript from the hand of Aaron ben Asher. Kept in St. Petersburg (formerly known as Leningrad), it forms the basis of modern printed Hebrew Bibles.

The standard printed Hebrew Bible used by translators is the *Biblia Hebraica Stuttgartensia*. The fourth edition appeared in 1977 (with amendments in 1983) and incorporated notes on variant readings, including those from the Dead Sea Scrolls (DSS, see pp. 208-9). A fifth edition is scheduled for 2005.

While the work of the Masoretes was truly remarkable, this still leaves us with manuscripts penned a minimum of one thousand years after the books of the Hebrew Bible were given recognition as Scripture and perhaps as long as two thousand years or more after some of the Old Testament was written. What are translators to do in those places where they are unsure of the reliability of the MT or when it makes little or no sense? Thankfully, we have other, older manuscripts, some in Hebrew and some in translation. Though not always more reliable, these often preserve the likely original better.

The Septuagint (LXX). From 323 B.C., Palestine and its Jewish population came under Greek-speaking control. Especially for the Jews who had left their homeland, a Greek translation of the Hebrew Bible was necessary. According to one account, this vital work was undertaken by seventy-two scholars and completed in just seventy-two days. And according to another, all seventy-two arrived at exactly the same translation!

In some Christian versions of the same tale it was seventy, not seventy-two, scholars who did the work. These rather fanciful explanations give us the name of this translation: Septuagint, from the Latin word for "seventy." The usual abbreviation is LXX (the Roman numeric symbol for seventy).

At first it was only the Torah, the part of the Hebrew Bible which Jews consider the most important, that was translated (in c. 250 B.C.). The remainder of the Hebrew Bible was translated over the next 150 years and was completed well before the time of Christ, though revisions were made later. New Testament writers often quote the LXX when referring to the Old Testament.

As well as containing the standard books of the Old Testament, the LXX also has the books of the Apocrypha. Not all of these have Hebrew originals; some were written in Greek from the start. As well as these extra books, the LXX contains significant additions to the books of Esther and Daniel. In contrast, the books of Job and Jeremiah are considerably shorter in their LXX versions than in the MT. All this points to the fact that the text of the Old Testament remained fluid prior to the time of Christ or even a little later.

The quality and reliability of the LXX translation is variable. In places it is very literal; in others very free. Many copies have been preserved, including fragments dating back as far as the second century B.C.

Nevertheless, translators must take care in how far they trust the LXX against the MT. Recent studies have shown that LXX differences from the MT are often the result of the former employing paraphrase rather than translating literally a supposed underlying Hebrew text that is more reliable than the MT. Where the MT is unclear or corrupt, however, the LXX can be very helpful to the translator, especially if there are other independent witnesses to the variant reading.

Other Greek translations of the Old Testament. Later, Greek translations are also useful to the translator. The most significant translations—by three Jewish scholars, Aquila, Symmachus and Theodotion—all appeared in the second century A.D. In c. A.D. 240 the Christian scholar Origen prepared a version of the Old Testament arranged in six parallel columns, the *Hexapla*. Alongside the Hebrew, he placed the Hebrew transliterated into Greek letters, the LXX, the three Greek translations noted above, and his own revision of the LXX.

The Dead Sea Scrolls. Alongside the MT and LXX, the most important source of information about the text of the Hebrew Bible is the Dead Sea Scrolls (DSS). Discovered in 1947 in a series of eleven caves just south of Jericho (called Qumran), they have been rightly described as the archaeological find of the twentieth century. One scroll turned out to be a complete copy of Isaiah dating from 150 B.C., more than a thousand years older than any previously known copy.

Altogether, the buried library was found to hold 25,000 fragments of ancient manuscripts. Scholars are still piecing them together! Fragments of all the OT books, with the exception of Esther, have been found at Qumran. None contains any vowels, just the consonantal Hebrew text. The manuscripts date from c. 250 B.C. to no later than A.D. 68, when the Essene community that gathered the library, came under attack. The DSS have been particularly helpful in our understanding of the text of Isaiah, Samuel, Psalms and Habakkuk.

The RSV was the first translation to take advantage of the discoveries made at Qumran. Later the NRSV added an entire paragraph to the end of 1 Samuel 10—verses not found in the MT. This addition helps

make sense of the story about Nahash the Ammonite with which
1 Samuel 11 abruptly begins.[1]

While interest naturally focuses on those places where the Qumran texts differ from the MT, it should be pointed out that the DSS
agree far more often with the MT than they disagree with it. Indeed,
around 60 percent of the total belong to a family of manuscripts from
which the MT is derived. More than anything else, the DSS underline
the reliability of the MT. Even though we have only tenth- and elev-
enth-century copies of the MT, it clearly rests on a much older text
tradition, one that has been transmitted and preserved with astonishing accuracy.

Other OT manuscripts. Alongside the manuscripts discussed
above, a few others are sometimes consulted by Old Testament scholars. Though less important than the MT, the LXX or the DSS, these are
listed here for the sake of completion.

- **The Samaritan Pentateuch.** The origin of the Samaritans is open to
  speculation, but by New Testament times they were a well-established group who followed their own form of the Jewish religion.
  The Samaritans had their own version of the Torah (or Pentateuch)
  that predates the MT. In about a third of its variants the Samaritan
  Pentateuch agrees with the LXX against the MT.

- **The Aramaic targums.** Aramaic was the everyday language spoken by Jesus. The targums began as an oral commentary on the Hebrew text, given in Aramaic for the benefit of those unfamiliar with
  the official Hebrew used in the synagogues. Eventually, from about
  the time of Christ, these targums were written down. Targums exist
  for the whole Old Testament except for the books of Ezra, Ne-
  hemiah and Daniel. The two targums most often consulted are *Targum Onkelos* and *Targum Jonathan*, covering the Pentateuch and
  Prophets respectively.

- **The Syriac Peshitta.** Just as the Hebrew Bible was translated into
  Greek (the LXX), so it was also translated into Syriac, probably in the
  first or second century A.D. Like the LXX, the Peshitta varies from

very literal to very free in its translation of the Hebrew. It often shows a familiarity with the LXX. The oldest Peshitta manuscripts go back to the fifth century A.D.

• **The Latin Vulgate.** In c. A.D. 380 the distinguished Christian scholar Jerome began a new Latin translation of the whole Bible, dedicating it to Pope Damasus. It was a great improvement on previous Old Latin versions. For the Old Testament, Jerome was careful to consult the Hebrew manuscripts available to him, not just the LXX. The Vulgate remained the standard Bible of the Western church for a millennium. The best-preserved and most reliable complete manuscript of the Vulgate is *Codex Amiatinus*, dating from A.D. 716. The most beautiful is undoubtedly the Lindisfarne Gospels (c. A.D. 715), now in the British Library, with an Anglo-Saxon interlinear gloss added in the tenth century (see p. 116).

TRANSMISSION: THE NEW TESTAMENT

Oddly, the oldest manuscripts we have of the Greek New Testament are considerably older than the copies of the MT we have for the Old Testament. There are extant copies of the complete New Testament from as early as the fourth century, and there are fragments going back much further, even to the second century.

Unlike Old Testament translators, their New Testament counterparts work from an eclectic text (i.e., a composite Greek text compiled from all the available manuscripts). There are two standard editions: one prepared by the United Bible Societies (4th edition, 1993, and generally referred to as UBS4); and one prepared by the scholars Eberhard Nestlé and Kurt Aland (27th edition, 1993, and referred to as NA27). The two are identical in wording but differ in punctuation and in their apparatuses (i.e., footnotes indicating variant readings).

When the AV/KJV was translated, the oldest and best Greek manuscripts had not yet been discovered. The earliest used by Erasmus for his 1516 edition of the Greek New Testament dates back no further than the tenth century. It was principally from Erasmus's Testament that Tyndale worked, and it was still the standard text when the translators of the AV/KJV began their task, though by then one late fifth-century manuscript, *Codex Bezae* (containing just the Gospels and Acts), had come to light. Other, even more significant Greek manuscripts are now available to New Testament scholars.

Codex Alexandrinus. An early fifth-century manuscript of almost the whole Bible (LXX and NT), the Codex Alexandrinus was presented to Charles I in 1627, just sixteen years after the publication of the AV/KJV. Parts of Matthew, John and 1 Corinthians are missing.

Codex Vaticanus. The chief treasure of the Vatican Library, where it was "found" by archaeologist Count Tischendorf in 1843, the Codex Vaticanus dates from the fourth century and contains the whole New Testament as far as 2 Thessalonians.

Codex Sinaiticus. A fourth-century Greek manuscript containing the whole of the New Testament and some of the LXX, the Codex Sinaiticus was discovered in 1844 in the monastery of St. Catherine on Mount Sinai by Lobegott Friedrich Konstantin von Tischendorf. Like the Codex Alexandrinus, it is now in the British Library.

All three of these codices are uncial manuscripts, meaning they are handwritten with large, capital letters. All are on parchment (i.e., animal skin). Earlier still than these codices are the papyri, small fragments of New Testament texts made from papyrus, manufactured by the crushing and drying of reeds. The first came to light in 1778; today over one hundred have been cataloged, the two most important collections being the Chester Beatty Papyri (discovered c. 1930) and the Bodmer Collection (1952).

In the former collection, the most significant is p45 (p = papyrus), containing the Gospels and Acts and dating from the early third century. In the same collection is p52, a much smaller fragment containing just four verses from John 18. Dated to c. A.D. 125, it is the oldest extant New Testament manuscript.[2]

As well as Greek manuscripts, New Testament translators occasionally make use of early Syriac and Coptic translations, as well as the Latin Vulgate (see p. 210).

TEXTUAL CRITICISM

It is one thing to have all these manuscripts available; it is another to know how to make sense of them. The science/art of textual criticism is by no means easy and often involves careful judgment and the balancing of probabilities.

Textual critics need to be aware of the kinds of error a scribe can make. Accidental errors include

- dittography: repeating a word or phrase, perhaps when the copyist's eye jumps back a line
- haplography: missing a letter, word or phrase, often when the copyist's eye jumps forward
- metathesis: transposing two letters to make a different word (as in *unite/untie*)
- misreading one letter for another (in Hebrew, for example, the letters "D" and "R" are very similar)
- mishearing one letter for another: applicable only when one scribe is writing at the dictation of another (in the New Testament, the pronouns "our" [Greek *hēmōn*, pronounced "hay-mone"] and "your" [*hymōn*, pronounced "hu-mone"] can be confused in this way; e.g., should 1 Jn 1:4 read "our joy" or "your joy"?)

Deliberate alterations include

- harmonization: deliberately bringing two texts into line (e.g., making a story from one Gospel agree with the same story in another Gospel)
- correction: making a substitution for a word or phrase that is not understood
- revision of spelling and grammar to make the text more polished

The starting point for most translators of the Old Testament is the MT. Only where this does not make good sense or seems corrupt do translators consult other sources such as the LXX.

In the absence of other manuscript evidence, scholars sometimes revert to the device of "conjectural emendation": taking an educated guess as to what the original Hebrew might have been. This generally involves attempting to make sense of the Hebrew consonants but with different vowels or word breaks. In the English sentence that follows, just moving one letter makes all the difference to its meaning:

• God is now here

• God is nowhere

During the mid-twentieth century the MT was not altogether trusted, and scholars were quicker than they are now to suggest emendations. The Old Testament translations in both the RSV and NEB have been criticized for departing too far from the MT.

A particular problem with the Old Testament is the large number of words found only once or twice in the whole Hebrew Bible, making it difficult to guess their precise meaning from the context. Knowing the meaning of a similar word in a cognate language can help. Alternatively, the way the word is translated in the LXX may give a clue, but sometimes the LXX translators made guesses too!

The task of the New Testament scholar is not necessarily any easier. There are some 5,500 Greek manuscripts to choose between, plus 20,000 more in other languages. Generally speaking, older is better. The textual critic also gives importance to the "family" to which an individual manuscript belongs. Several such families, each coming from a particular region, are generally recognized, among them Alexandrian (Egypt), Western (Rome) and Byzantine (Turkey). The Byzantine family of texts, on which the AV/KJV was mostly based, is now regarded as inferior to the other two. The Alexandrian is preferred to the Western.

There are certain general rules that scholars follow in ascertaining the best text. For example, where a text seems to have been altered deliberately, it is probable that the shorter variant is correct. Scribes were more likely to add an explanatory comment than make a deletion. However, in cases of accidental error such as omission by haplography, the longer text is more probable. Another tenet of textual criticism is that a reading which is harder to understand is more likely to be original than one that is easier: scribes often tried to clarify or smooth out a difficult text.

Textual criticism is a specialized subject; only a brief introduction has been given here. A translation's preface will indicate how to make sense of footnotes showing variant readings, and should always be read carefully. Refer to the bibliography for further information about textual criticism.

DISPUTED PASSAGES

Certain New Testament passages are included in some Bibles but not in others. The principal ones are discussed here

The endings of Mark's Gospel. Mark's Gospel has three possible endings: an abrupt ending at 16:8, the so-called longer ending, comprising verses 9-20, and a shorter ending of just a few lines.

The longer ending is missing from the earliest Greek manuscripts but was probably in circulation by the second century. Several manuscripts which do contain it point out that it is a later addition. Though it is not written by Mark, many accept it as historical; the stories it contains are mostly paralleled in at least one of the other Gospels. For example, verses 12-13 are an abbreviated account of Jesus' appearance on the road to Emmaus, recorded in Luke 24.

The shorter ending, however, is of a much later date, appearing in a fourth- or fifth-century Latin manuscript and in no Greek manuscripts before the seventh century. Like the longer ending, its style is different from the rest of Mark's Gospel.

The woman caught in adultery (Jn 7:53—8:11). The delightful story of forgiveness about a woman caught in adultery is not included in manuscripts of John's Gospel earlier than the sixth century. Manuscripts that do include it place it after various points in the text: John 7:36; 7:44; 7:52 (its traditional place); and even Luke 21:38. Its style and wording are different from other parts of John's Gospel, and placed where it is, it seems to interrupt the original writer's flow of thought.

However, there is no reason to doubt the historical nature of the story; it is too scandalous to have been made up. Neither is there any reason to reject it from the canon of Scripture. It has a ring of truth.

While it is not written by John, we need not doubt it is based on fact and inspired by the Holy Spirit.

The ending of the Lord's Prayer (Mt 6:13). The familiar ending to the Lord's Prayer—"For yours is the kingdom, the power and the glory, Amen"—is omitted from almost all modern Bibles. The words do not appear in any Greek manuscript earlier than the fifth century. It was almost certainly added by later copyists who wrote back into the Gospel the words of the prayer as it had developed over time in regular church use. The words are not part of Matthew's Gospel, nor do they appear at all in any manuscript, at any date, of Luke's parallel account (Lk 11:1-4). The early church's liturgical addition is scriptural, however; the words are taken from 1 Chronicles 29:11-13.

The Johannine Comma (1 Jn 5:7). The AV/KJV renders 1 John 5:6-8 as follows:

> ⁶This is he that came by water and blood, even Jesus Christ; not by water only, but by water and blood. And it is the Spirit that beareth witness, because the Spirit is truth.
>
> ⁷For there are three that bear record *in heaven, the Father, the Word, and the Holy Ghost: and these three are one.*
>
> ⁸*And there are three that bear witness in earth,* the spirit, and the water, and the blood: and these three agree in one.

Almost all modern Bibles since 1900 leap from halfway through verse 7 to the middle of verse 8, omitting the words identified here in italics. Many in the AV/KJV-only school protest, arguing that the missing words represent one of the Bible's best proof-texts for the doctrine of the Trinity. The words, however, do not appear in any manuscript prior to the sixth century and then only in Latin; nor are they found in any Greek manuscript earlier than the twelfth century. In all likelihood, the phrase was first added by way of a marginal note written by a commentator; a later copyist then included it in the actual text of the letter, attracted no doubt by the reference to the Trinity. Modern Bibles quite rightly omit the phrase or relegate it to a footnote: it is not part of canonical Scripture.

APPENDIX 2

OTHER TWENTIETH-
AND TWENTY-FIRST-CENTURY
TRANSLATIONS

This appendix lists some of the lesser-known but still significant English translations to have been published in the last seventy years. No attempt to present an exhaustive list has been made. Even if desirable, such a task would be next to impossible. Some of the following translations may not be available in American editions.

Charles B. Williams (1937)

In *The NT in the Language of the People*, Greek professor Charles B. Williams attempted to bring out every last nuance of the Greek New Testament tenses. He was generally unsuccessful, though some passages, according to F. F. Bruce, have "real power."[1]

The Bible in Basic English (1949)

Intended for those whose second language is English, this Bible employs a strictly limited vocabulary of 850 words devised by semanticist C. K. Ogden of Cambridge University. The actual translation was prepared by a committee working under Samuel Henry Hooke of London, who added a further fifty special Bible words and a further one hundred deemed the most helpful in reading English poetic verse. The New Testament appeared in 1941, the complete Bible in 1949.

C. K. Williams's New Testament in Plain English (1952)

Undertaken by Charles Kingsley Williams, C. K. Williams's New Testament is similar to *The Bible in Basic English* (see above), but with a vocabulary limited to 1,500 words. It is published in London by SPCK.

E. V. Rieu (1952)

Classical Greek scholar Emil Rieu (1887-1972) is best known for his translation of Homer's *Iliad* and *Odyssey*, but he also attempted a successful translation of *The Four Gospels*, published in the Penguin Classics in 1952. His translation is best described as moderately meaning-driven in approach but formal in style.

A BBC radio broadcast in 1953, in which E. V. Rieu and J. B. Phillips were interviewed side by side, makes for interesting reflection. Rieu describes his approach as one of "equivalent effect." His aim was to produce a translation "which comes nearest to giving its modern audience the same effect as the original had on its first audience."[2] This is a very early statement of the principle of meaning-driven translation.

The Authentic New Testament: Hugh Schonfield (1955)

A version of the New Testament from a distinctly Jewish perspective, Schonfield's translation approaches the text "as if [these documents] had recently been recovered from a cave in Palestine or beneath the sands of Egypt, and had never previously been given to the public." Notes supply helpful information on Jewish references in the New Testament. Schonfield died in 1988.

Wuest's Expanded New Testament (1961)

Kenneth Wuest endeavored to reproduce every shade and nuance of the Greek text. The result is a rather overdone translation.

Richard Lattimore: New Testament (1962-1982)

This simple, literal rendering by a classical Greek scholar aims to reflect the style of the original in an English translation. It was first published posthumously in one volume in 1996 in the United States (1998 in Britain). Lattimore died in 1984.

The Anchor Bible (1964)

The Anchor Bible translation is associated with the famous Anchor commentary series. Different books were prepared by different translators.

Alan T. Dale (1967 and 1972)

Dale, a teacher, published *New World: The Heart of the New Testament in Plain English* in 1968, and *Winding Quest: The Heart of the Old Testament in Plain English* in 1972. Both are abridged paraphrases written for classroom use and were widely acclaimed in their day.

Cotton Patch Version (1968)

Prepared by Clarence Jordan, founder of the Koinonia Community, Georgia, this paraphrase employs the dialect of the farming community of the American South but was brought to prominence by an influential Broadway show (see also pp. 39-40).

William Barclay: New Testament (1968-1969)

A meaning-driven translation by a highly respected Scottish clergyman, scholar and broadcaster, Barclay's New Testament was published originally in two parts in 1968 (the Gospels and Acts) and 1969 (Letters and Revelation). His translation work was first seen in his seventeen-volume *Daily Study Bible*, published between 1954 and 1957. Barclay died in 1978.

The Translator's New Testament (1973)

A specialist version of the New Testament was prepared by the British and Foreign Bible Society to help Bible translators without a knowledge of Greek to carry out their task. Generally simple in style and vocabulary, it is now used less often: many translators on the mission field prefer the NET Bible (see pp. 195-96) for this purpose. An attempt to prepare a *Translator's Old Testament* has never been completed.

Peter Levi (1976)

Also published in the Penguin Classic series under the general editorship of E. V. Rieu (see above) is *The Psalms* by Jesuit priest and fellow classicist Peter Levi (b. 1931). The moderately form-driven translation is from the Hebrew, not the Latin. Levi also wrote *The English Bible 1534-1859*.

J. P. Green (1982 and 1987)

In 1982 J. P. Green made a revision of the AV/KJV called the King James 2 Version. It should not be confused with the NKJV, discussed on pages 162-63. Based on this, Green went on in 1987 to produce *A Literal Translation of the Bible*. Emphasizing the verbal nature of biblical inspiration, Green's translation is almost as literal (and as incomprehensible) as Robert Young's in 1862 (see p. 39). It is now available as a purportedly scholarly interlinear Bible, together with the Hebrew and Greek text.

Green renders Mark 6:21 thus: "And a suitable day having come, when Herod on his birth-feast made a supper for his great ones, and the chiliarchs, and the first ones of Galilee . . ."[3]

Tanakh or New Jewish Version (1985)

In 1917 the Jewish Publication Society of America published *The Holy Scriptures According to the Masoretic Text*. With some affinity to the AV/KJV and employing a form-driven approach, this became the standard Jewish translation for the next half century.

An entirely fresh translation was undertaken in three stages: the Torah in 1962-1963, the Prophets in 1978 and the Writings in 1982. The New Jewish Version, though also published by the Jewish Publication Society, uses far less "Bible English" than the 1917 version, moving as it does toward a meaning-driven style and representing a considerable modernization. A one-volume edition titled *Tanakh* (an acronym for *tôrâ, nêbî᾿îm* and *kětûbîm*—the Law, Prophets and Writings respectively—the three parts of the Hebrew Bible) was issued in 1985. A Hebrew-English parallel edition appeared in 1999.

Sakae Kubo and Walter Specht say of the NJV:

> The NJV is a monument to careful scholarship, particularly in dealing with the traditional Hebrew text. Its fidelity to that text is unquestionable. Combined with it is a concern to break away from the traditional English translations and produce a version that is clothed in contemporary idiomatic English. In both of these attempts, the version is successful. It ranks as one of the best translations of the Hebrew Bible available.[4]

Cassirer's New Testament (1989)

Heinz Cassirer, a German-born Jew, came to live in England and was baptized an Anglican in 1955. His translation, titled *God's New Covenant: A New Testament Translation*, was edited, prefaced and published after Cassirer's death by his former secretary Ronald Weitzman. Its interest lies in the fact that it was undertaken by a Jewish academic who had never read any of the New Testament before reaching the age of forty-nine.

New Life Version (1993)

A children's version first published as *The Children's New Testament* in 1966 for Eskimo children just beginning to read, the New Life Version uses a limited vocabulary. It is now published in several editions, including Baker Book House's *Precious Moments Children's Bible* (1993).

The 21st Century King James Version (1994)

Retired attorney William Prindele has updated the language of the AV/KJV in accordance with guidelines derived from *Webster's New International Dictionary*. Where Webster indicates an AV/KJV word to be archaic, Prindele has updated it. Like the translators of the NKJV (pp. 162-63), Prindele has not taken into account the biblical manuscripts discovered more recently than those underlying the AV/KJV. He is now working on *The Third Millennium Bible*, complete with the Apocrypha.

Everett Fox (1995)

A Jewish translation of the five books of Moses, Fox's aim is stated in the preface:

> The purpose of this work is to draw the reader into the world of the Hebrew Bible through the power of its language. While this sounds simple enough, it is not usually possible in translation. Indeed, the premise of almost all Bible translations, past and present, is that the meaning of the text should be conveyed in as

clear and comfortable a manner as possible in one's own language. Yet the truth is that the Bible was not written in the English of the twentieth or even the seventeenth century; it is ancient, sometimes obscure, and speaks in a way quite different from ours. Accordingly, I have sought here primarily to echo the style of the original, believing that the Bible is best approached, at least at the beginning, on its own terms. . . . The result looks and sounds very different from what we are accustomed to encountering as the Bible, whether in the much-loved grandeur of the King James version or the clarity and easy fluency of the many recent attempts.

There is more praise on the dust jacket:

This new translation re-creates the full force of the Bible's original rhetoric in poetry—its rhythms, nuances, and stylistic devices. . . . This new English translation restores the poetics of the Hebrew original—the echoes, allusions, alliteration, and wordplays that rhetorically underscore its meaning and are intrinsic to a text meant to be read aloud and heard.

Fox's translation has been praised by former British poet laureate Ted Hughes: "For once since the King James, a translation that comes right out of the heart of the living culture of the thing." Work continues with translating other parts of the Hebrew Bible. When complete, it will be known as the Schocken Bible.

Stern's Complete Jewish Bible (1998)
Like Cassirer, David Stern (b. 1935) is a Jewish convert to Christianity. His New Testament appeared in 1989, his Old Testament in 1998. The Old Testament was based on the standard Jewish translation of 1917. Many Hebrew words and spellings are kept by Stern, for instance *talmîdîm* for "disciples." Jesus is called *Yeshua*.

The 21st Century New Testament (1998)
A dual translation of the New Testament in two parallel columns—one

with a highly literal translation, one with a moderately free rendering—the 21st Century New Testament was published for the new millennium by Insight Press, Bristol, England.

The Biker's Bible (2001 and later)

An American paraphrase by Dan Sindlinger, the Biker's Bible is aimed at "busy people on the move." The Gospels of Matthew and Mark appeared in 2001. By 2003, the letters of Romans, Galatians, Ephesians, James and John had been added. Sindlinger was formerly a Bible translator for six years among the Gola people of Liberia and for ten years among the Lakota people of South Dakota. Further details are available at <www.geocities.com/better_life_publications>.

The Street Bible (2003)

A street-language paraphrase by Rob Lacey, the Street Bible is written for the young urban reader and designed to make an impact when heard. It was first presented at Spring Harvest, the popular British Christian festival, in 2003.

The Recovery Bible (NT 1974, revised 1991; OT 2003)

The Recovery Bible is the work of an editorial team representing the Californian-based Living Stream Ministry, dedicated to promoting the distinctive teachings of the Chinese Christian leader and writer Watchman Nee (d. 1972) and his student Witness Lee. The Recovery Bible is distinguished by its interpretive outlines, footnotes, charts and marginal references, all reflecting the group's theological outlook. The notes aside, the translation itself is rather good, taking a form-driven but not overly literal approach.

The New Testament was translated by an editorial team and first published in 1974; a revision followed in 1991. It is also available in Chinese, Spanish, Russian, Japanese and several other languages. All the annotations are the work of Witness Lee. A complete English Bible was published in 1999; one with footnotes and cross-references in 2003. More information is available at <www.recoveryversion.org>.

Good as New: A Radical Retelling of the Scriptures (2004), edited by John Henson

This offering, coordinated and edited by John Henson for the non-orthodox ONE Community for Christian Exploration, contains nineteen books of the New Testament together with the apocryphal Gospel of Thomas. It is aimed at non-Christians and is intended to communicate with those who have little or no prior knowledge of the Christian faith. Its style is colloquial and deliberately shocking. The Son of Man becomes "The Complete Person," the Father our "Loving God" or "Parent," and the Holy Spirit is referred to as "she." While some might regard it as an imaginative paraphrase, the subtitle—*A Radical Retelling*—is the more apt description. Enough said.

APPENDIX 3

INTERNET RESOURCES

HANDHELD SOFTWARE

Three very popular programs available for PDAs (Personal Digital Assistants) are *My Bible!* from Laridian Software, *Bible Reader* from Olive-Tree and *Bible with You* from GMPSoft Ltd. All three offer a good number of translations. The respective websites are <www.laridian.com>, <www.olivetree.com> and <www.gmpsoft.com>.

DESKTOP SOFTWARE

It is a little risky attempting to list the various Bible software programs available; the number is growing all the time. Several companies provide a basic search-engine with a variety of translations, commentaries, dictionaries, original-language tools and other books that can be purchased as add-ons in various price ranges. Well-established names include WordSearch, Libronix (formerly Logos), Quick Verse, Bible-Works, Zondervan's NIV Bible, Study Library, eBible, Gramcord, Accordance, iLumina and Compton's Interactive NIV.

WEBSITES

General sites, giving access to several translations, include

- www.gospelcom.net
- www.bible-researcher.com
- www.geocities.com/bible_translation
- www.tyndale.cam.ac.uk

Sites relating to specific versions include

- RSV and NRSV: www.ncccusa.org/newbtu/btuhome.html

- ESV: www.gnpcb.org/home/ESV
- NASB: www.gospelcom.net/lockman/nasb
- Amp.: www.gospelcom.net/lockman/amplified
- NASB and Amplified: www.studybibleforum.com/bibletext.php
- NET Bible: www.bible.org/netbible
- ISV: http://isv.org
- NLT: www.newlivingtranslation.com
- NIV: www.gospelcom.net/ibs/niv/index.php
- TNIV: www.tniv.info
- NAB: www.nccbuscc.org/nab
- GW: www.godsword.org
- *The Message*: www.navpress.com/BibleProducts
- AV/KJV, NKJV, ASV, NASB: http://bible.lifeway.com
- WEB: www.ebible.org/bible/web
- Biker Bible: www.geocities.com/better_life_publications/biker.html
- Recovery Version: www.recoveryversion.org
- CEV: www.americanbible.org
- HSCB: http://hcsb.broadmanholman.com/crossmain.asp or http://bible.lifeway.com/crossmain.asp

NOTES

Introduction

[1] The TNIV New Testament was published in April 2002; the ESV in May 2002; the completed version of Eugene Peterson's *The Message* in July of the same year; and the HCSB in April 2004. Forthcoming translations and updates due in 2004-2005 are listed on p. 201.

[2] Certain translations are not dealt with in this book: translations of a sectarian nature (the Watchtower New World Translation is the sole exception), very short-lived versions, story Bibles, dialect translations, privately published translations, those with a limited circulation and those prepared as part of a commentary. Jewish translations are given in appendix two.

Chapter One: The Translator's Art

[1] The inspiration of Scripture and the different books it contains are discussed in my earlier book, *The Bible Unwrapped* (Milton Keynes, U.K.: Scripture Union, 2001).

[2] Aramaic is confined mainly to Ezra and Daniel and amounts to no more than a dozen chapters in all. It was also the language spoken by Jesus, and there are a few isolated Aramaic words in the New Testament.

[3] "The noblest monument of English prose" was reputedly said of the AV/KJV by Robert Lowth (1710-1787), professor of poetry at Oxford University. See Alister McGrath, *In the Beginning: The Story of the King James Bible* (London: Hodder & Stoughton, 2001), p. 278.

[4] The reader might like to compare the following verses in the AV/KJV with a modern translation: Ps 26:2; 73:21; Jer 11:20; 17:10; 20:12.

[5] Mark's fast-paced style and use of the so-called "historic present" may reflect the fact that his principal source, Peter, was an eyewitness to the events described. Where Mark uses the present tense, Matthew and Luke employ the past.

[6] Moisés Silva, quoted in Glen Scorgie et al., eds., *The Challenge of Bible Translation* (Grand Rapids: Zondervan, 2003), p. 52.

[7] D. A. Carson comments on this point in ibid., pp. 102-3.

[8] Kevin G. Smith, *Bible Translation and Relevance*, DLitt thesis, University of Stellenbosch, South Africa, December 2000.

[9] Sectarian versions such as the New World Translation (pp. 149-50) and agenda-driven translations like the New Testament and Psalms Inclusive Version (pp. 172-73) contain significant inaccuracies.

[10]Some might argue that the Holy Spirit can reveal to later readers a meaning that the original human author never foresaw, for instance in the future fulfillment of prophecy. While this is true, it is not the translator's task to offer such exegesis, but only to make a faithful translation.

Chapter Two: Word-for-Word or Meaning-for-Meaning?

[1]It was a bone of contention for evangelicals that the translators of the RSV changed "propitiation" into "expiation." See p. 146.

[2]*Concordance* as consistent translation of a particular word should not be confused with *a* concordance, or index, of Bible words.

[3]Mark Strauss, *Distorting Scripture?* (Downers Grove, Ill.: InterVarsity Press, 1998), pp. 96-97.

[4]In "Dog bites man," *dog* is the subject and *man* the object.

[5]Tony Payne, quoted in articles on the ESV at <www.matthiasmedia.com.au/ESV>, some of which have also been published in the journal *The Briefing*.

[6]Grammatically speaking, a metaphor and a simile are different: "God is a rock" is a metaphor; "God is *like* a rock" and "God is *as strong as* a rock" are similes.

[7]Such a phrase, familiar to ranchers, is unfamiliar outside of that context.

[8]Gordon D. Fee and Douglas Stuart, *How to Read the Bible for All Its Worth* (Grand Rapids: Zondervan, 2003), p. 42.

[9]Fee, "Reflections on Commentary Writing," in *Listening to the Spirit in the Text* (Grand Rapids: Eerdmans, 2000), p. 18.

[10]Ibid. Some of Fee's preferred choices have now found their way into the TNIV, a revision of the NIV.

[11]This example is further discussed by Gerald Hammond in Robert Alter and Frank Kermode, eds., *The Literary Guide to the Bible* (London: Collins, 1987), pp. 654-55.

[12]Some have attempted to make an objective assessment of where translations lie on a spectrum of literalness; see, e.g., Robert L. Thomas, *How to Choose a Bible Version* (Fearn, Ross-shire, U.K.: Christian Focus, 2000), chap. 3.

Chapter Three: A Question of Style

[1]For the fascinating story of the Bible as a book see Christopher de Hamel, *The Book* (London: Phaidon, 2001).

[2]See, for instance, the example on pp. 63-64 on the use of repetition in Hebrew for effect.

[3]For the mathematically minded, the formula for the Flesch-Kincaid test is as follows: $(ASL30.39) + (ASW311.8) - 15.59$. ASL is the average sentence length in words; ASW is the average number of syllables per word. Scores above a grade level of 12 are not computed as they have little real meaning.

[4]William Wonderly, *Bible Translations for Popular Use* (London: United Bible Societies, 1968), pp. 38-40.

[5]Even the apostle Peter found some of Paul's letters hard to understand! See 2 Pet 3:16.

[6]For a full discussion of translation style see Cecil Hargreaves, *A Translator's Freedom* (Sheffield, U.K.: Sheffield Academic Press, 1993).

[7]One slight advantage of thee/thou language is that in translations which employ it, it is possible to distinguish between second person singular and plural: in the AV/KJV, "Thou" and "Thee" are singular (employed, respectively, for the subject and object of a verb) while the corresponding plurals are "Ye" and "You." In modern English, "you" embraces the usage of all four pronouns.

[8]Barclay M. Newman et al., *Creating and Crafting the Contemporary English Version* (New York: American Bible Society, 1996), p. 36.

[9]David Hallamshire, *The Yorkshire Bible Stories* (Sheffield, U.K.: Fleming Press, 1991).

[10]Examples taken from Newman, *Creating and Crafting*, p. 76.

[11]One widely held view of the Synoptic Gospels is that Mark was written first; Matthew and Luke copied from him and a further common source, generally referred to as Q.

[12]Though the translators of the AV/KJV employed a new line for every verse, Tyndale, Coverdale and Matthew's Bible all used paragraphs.

[13]Romans 1:4 is rendered as "Spirit," without a footnote, by the RSV, the ESV and the TNIV.

Chapter Four: His and Hers: Gender Accuracy

[1]Mark Strauss, *Distorting Scripture?* (Downers Grove, Ill.: InterVarsity Press, 1998), pp. 13-14.

[2]Mark Strauss, in *The Challenge of Bible Translation,* ed. Glen G. Scorgie et al. (Grand Rapids: Zondervan, 2003), p. 115.

[3]The phrase "children of Israel" appears almost six hundred times in the AV/KJV. The NASB has "children of Israel" on one occasion (Deut 1:3); the AV/KJV has 'children of Israel' on all but four justifiable occasions: Gen 43:5; 46:5; Deut 23:17; 1 Chron 2:1.

[4]See, e.g., the footnote to Rom 1:13 ESV.

[5]See pp. 48-50 for the debate on translating according to simple dictionary definition or according to context.

[6]Strauss, *Distorting Scripture?* p. 205.

[7]Ibid., pp. 203-4.

[8]The TNIV's approach to translating *ioudaioi* is taken from the TNIV website: <www.tniv.info/bible/sample.php>. Italics in this quotation are in the original.

[9]For a fuller explanation of the CEV's policy on translating *ioudaioi* see Barclay M. Newman et al., *Creating and Crafting the Contemporary English Version* (New York: American Bible Society, 1996), pp. 62-64.

[10]One translation that takes political correctness to an extreme is *The New Testament and Psalms: An Inclusive Version,* discussed on pp. 172-73.

Chapter Five: Yet More Choices

[1]William Tyndale used "senior" in his 1526 New Testament, but changed this to "elder" in his 1534 edition.

[2]Strictly speaking, the Roman Catholic Church accepts all but three books of the Protestant Apocrypha as *deuterocanonical,* meaning "in a secondary canon." These exceptions are *First and Second Esdras* and the *Prayer of Manasseh,* which are not included in Roman Catholic Bibles.

[3]*The Catechism of the Roman Catholic Church*, paragraph 138.

[4]Bruce Metzger et al., *The Making of the New Revised Standard Version of the Bible* (Grand Rapids: Eerdmans, 1991), p. 62.

[5]Only some Bibles have section headings, but all translations have chapter breaks. Like section headings, these do not always fall where the flow of the text demands.

[6]The *NIV Thematic Study Bible* should not be confused with the popular *NIV Study Bible*.

[7]See my book *The Bible Unwrapped* (Milton Keynes, U.K.: Scripture Union, 2001). Chaps. 5 and 9 offer advice on study Bibles, concordances and using cross-references, together with worked examples.

Chapter Six: From Unauthorized to Authorized

[1]Bede *Ecclesiastical History of the English People* 4.24.

[2]There were three main dialects of Anglo-Saxon: Mercian, Northumbrian and West Saxon.

[3]Some accounts say Bede got no further than John 6:9; others suggest that he translated "a great part of the Bible."

[4]David Daniell gives an excellent account of Wycliffe and his Bibles in *The Bible in English* (New Haven, Conn.: Yale University Press, 2003), chap. 5.

[5]The first printed Bible was Gutenberg's 42-line Latin Bible, printed by him in Mainz, Germany, in 1456. However, printed Bibles did not become affordable until c. 1520, as new, movable-type technology spread.

[6]An account of Tyndale's debate from John Foxe's *Book of Martyrs*, cited in F. F. Bruce, *History of the Bible in English* (Cambridge: Lutterworth, 1979), p. 29. The language has been modernized.

[7]Only two complete copies of this first edition survive today. Bristol Baptist College paid a million pounds to the British Library for one copy, which served as the centerpiece of a special exhibition in 1994 to mark the five hundredth anniversary of Tyndale's birth.

[8]David Daniell, *Tyndale's New Testament* (New Haven, Conn.: Yale University Press, 1989).

[9]Bruce Metzger, *The Bible in Translation* (Grand Rapids: Baker, 2001), p. 59.

[10]Cf. Brian Moynahan, *If God Spare My Life* (London: Little, Brown, 2002).

[11]Daniell, *Bible in English*, pp. 219ff.

[12]Gerald Hammond, *The Making of the English Bible* (Manchester, U.K.: Carcanet Press, 1982), p. 143.

[13]"Appointed" did not have the meaning to sixteenth century readers that it does today. It has little to do with authorization but simply meant that the pages were furnished with features which made it suitable for public reading. Today, one might similarly talk of a well-appointed kitchen.

[14]Moynahan, *If God Spare My Life*, p. 1.

[15]Metzger, *Bible in Translation*, pp. 76-77.

[16]Examples of idiomatic translation in the AV/KJV include the phrases "God save the king" (1 Sam 10:24), "The theives . . . cast the same in his teeth" (Mt 27:44) and "God forbid" (Rom 6:2, 15; 7:7, 13 and elsewhere).

Chapter Seven: Crossing the Centuries

[1]F. F. Bruce, *History of the Bible in English* (Cambridge: Lutterworth, 1979), p. 138.

[2]Ibid., p. 142.

[3]Ibid.

[4]C. H. Spurgeon, quoted in Luther A. Weigle, ed., *An Introduction to the Revised Standard Version of the New Testament* (Nashville: Nelson, 1946), pp. 11-12.

[5]Bruce, *History of the Bible in English*, p. 144.

[6]Ibid., pp. 139-40.

[7]Ibid., pp. 167, 171.

[8]Bruce praises Gerrit Verkuyl's work and draws some interesting comparisons with the RSV. See Bruce, *History of the Bible in English*, pp. 229-34.

Chapter Eight: A New Era Begins

[1]F. F. Bruce, *History of the Bible in English* (Cambridge: Lutterworth, 1979), p. 187.

[2]David Daniell, *The Bible in English* (New Haven, Conn.: Yale University Press, 2003), pp. 739, 840 n. 94.

[3]Changes to the RSV included Gospel references relating to Mary: "favored one" becomes "full of grace" in Lk 1:28; Joseph is told to "send her away" rather than "divorce her" in Mt 1:19; Jesus' "brothers" become Jesus' "brethren" (on the grounds that this somehow preserved the Catholic doctrine of the perpetual virginity of Mary). In addition, endnotes on doctrinal matters were added in accordance with Catholic canon law.

[4]For a more detailed explanation of "expiation" versus "propitiation", see I. H. Marshall et al., eds., *New Bible Dictionary,* 3rd ed. (Downers Grove, Ill.: InterVarsity Press, 1996), pp. 353, 975.

[5]Bruce Metzger, *The Bible in Translation* (Grand Rapids: Baker, 2001), p. 120; for more on the controversy surrounding the RSV, see Peter J. Thuesen, *In Discordance with the Scriptures* (New York: Oxford University Press, 1999), esp. chap. 4.

[6]The NEB, in fact, deviates further from the standard Hebrew Old Testament text than the RSV and, in several places, rearranges the verse order within certain Old Testament passages.

[7]Metzger, *Bible in Translation*, p. 133.

[8]Further details of the NEB's philosophy of presentation are given in Geoffrey Hunt, ed., *About the New English Bible* (Oxford and Cambridge: Oxford University Press/Cambridge University Press, 1970), pp. 40-55.

[9]In Greek the definite article "the" is routinely dropped after the verb "to be."

[10]J. B. Phillips, *Ring of Truth* (London: Hodder & Stoughton, 1967), p. 17.

[11]Bruce, *History of the Bible in English*, p. 223.

[12]In 1963 Bishop John Robinson's *Honest to God* (London: SCM Press) fueled a debate over attitudes toward Christian belief and the reliability of the Bible. For a firsthand account of Phillips's life and work see Edwin H. Robertson, *Makers of the English Bible* (Cambridge: Lutterworth, 1990), pp. 206-13.

[13]Robertson, *Making of the English Bible*, p. 9.

[14]Bruce, *History of the Bible in English*, p. 208.
[15]Metzger, *Bible in Translation*, p. 128.

Chapter Nine: Formative Years: The 1970s and 1980s
[1]Sakae Kubo and Walter Specht, *So Many Versions?* (Grand Rapids: Zondervan, 1975), p. 199.
[2]One inquiry into an evangelical edition of the RSV was made by the Evangelical Theological Society, the other by Oaks Hills Christian Training School, Minnesota. See Peter J. Thuesen, *In Discordance with the Scriptures* (New York: Oxford University Press, 1999), p. 134.
[3]Kubo and Specht, *So Many Versions?*, p. 199.
[4]*The Story of the New International Version* (Colorado Springs: International Bible Society, 1978), p. 13, quoted in Kenneth Barker, *The Balance of the NIV* (Grand Rapids: Baker, 1999), p. 48.
[5]Robert Martin, *Accuracy of Translation* (1989; reprint London: Banner of Truth, 1997).
[6]Kenneth Barker, *Accuracy Defined and Illustrated* (Colorado Springs: International Bible Society, 1995).
[7]Steven M. Sheeley and Robert N. Nash Jr., *The Bible in English* (Nashville: Abingdon, 1997), pp. 50-51.

Chapter Ten: Old Faces in New Guises
[1]The full story of the REB is told in Roger Coleman, *New Light and Truth* (Oxford and Cambridge: Oxford University Press/Cambridge University Press, 1989).
[2]Examples of updates to the RSV in table 10.1 are taken from Bruce Metzger, *The Bible in Translation* (Grand Rapids: Baker, 2001), pp. 157-61, where many further illustrations can be found. A review of the NRSV in comparison with the RSV is offered by Sakae Kubo in the *Andrews University Seminary Studies* 29, no. 1 (1991): 61-69.
[3]Mark Strauss, *Distorting Scripture?* (Downers Grove, Ill.: InterVarsity Press, 1998), pp. 44-46.
[4]Ibid., p. 46.
[5]Examples of updates to the NIV in the CEV in table 10.2 are cited from Barclay M. Newman et al., *Creating and Crafting the Contemporary English Version* (New York: American Bible Society, 1996), p. 28.
[6]Such a claim is made in the NLT *Text and Product Preview* (Wheaton, Ill.: Tyndale House, 1996).

Chapter Eleven: Into a New Millennium
[1]So stated in an IBS press release on May 27, 1997.
[2]Craig Blomberg, in the online *Denver Journal* 6 (2003): 6:204.
[3]In fact, uses of singular *they/them* can be found in Shakespeare and even the AV/KJV. In the latter, Philippians 2:3 reads, "*Let* nothing *be done* through strife or vainglory; but in lowliness of mind let each esteem others better than themselves."
[4]There was, in the first beta edition of the NET Bible, a curious misprint. Proverbs 2:16

warns against "the sexually loose woman," but the notes accompanying this verse include a telephone number! The editor in question would have us believe he just happened to jot down a business number he wanted to remember while working on the notes for this verse, which then got incorporated into the printed Bible.

Chapter Twelve: Reflections and Conclusions

[1]*The Alternative Service Book 1980:* Collect for the Second Sunday in Advent.

Appendix One: Being Original

[1]See Bruce Metzger et al., *The Making of the New Revised Standard Version of the Bible* (Grand Rapids: Eerdmans, 1991), pp. 25-26, for a more detailed discussion of the added paragraph in 1 Samuel 11.

[2]Carsten Peter Thiede believes that a fragment from the seventh Qumran cave is from Mark's Gospel and can be dated to before A.D. 68. This claim, however, is disputed.

Appendix Two: Other Twentieth- and Twenty-First-Century Translations

[1]F. F. Bruce, *History of the Bible in English* (Cambridge: Lutterworth, 1979), p. 183.

[2]The interview was transcribed in *Bible Translator* 6 (1955): 153.

[3]Mark 6:21, from J. P. Green's *A Literal Translation of the Bible,* cited in Alan S. Duthie, *How to Choose Your Bible Wisely* (Carlisle, U.K.: Paternoster/Bible Society, 1995), p. 57.

[4]Sakae Kubo and Walter Specht, *So Many Versions?* rev. ed. (Grand Rapids: Zondervan, 1983), p. 143.

BIBLIOGRAPHY

The Bible in English: History (General)

Bruce, F. F. *History of the Bible in English*. 3rd ed. Cambridge: Lutterworth Press, 1979.

Daniell, David. *The Bible in English*. London: Yale University Press, 2003.

Hammond, Gerald. *The Making of the English Bible*. Manchester, U.K.: Carcanet Press, 1982.

Levi, Peter. *The English Bible 1534-1859*. London: Constable & Co., 1974.

Robertson, Edwin H. *Makers of the English Bible*. Cambridge: Lutterworth Press, 1990.

Vance, Laurence M. *A Brief History of English Bible Translations*. Pensacola, Fla.: Vance Publications, 2000.

The Bible in English: History (with a Special Focus on Tyndale/KJV)

Bobrick, Benson. *The Making of the English Bible*. London: Weidenfeld & Nicholson, 2001.

Daniell, David. *Let There Be Light: William Tyndale and the Making of the English Bible*. London: British Library, 1994.

McGrath, Alister. *In the Beginning: The Story of the King James Bible*. London: Hodder & Stoughton, 2001.

Malles, Stanley, and Jeffrey McQuain. *Coined by God: Words and Phrases That First Appear in the English Translations of the Bible*. New York: W. W. Norton, 2003.

Moynahan, Brian. *If God Spare My Life*. London: Little, Brown & Co., 2002.

The Bible in English: Guides

Bratcher, Robert. "Paraphrases." In *The Oxford Companion to the Bible*, edited by B. M. Metzger and M. D. Coogan. Oxford: Oxford University Press, 1993.

Comfort, Philip W. *The Essential Guide to Bible Versions*. Wheaton, Ill.: Tyndale House, 2000.

Duthie, Alan S. *How to Choose Your Bible Wisely*. 2nd ed. Carlisle, U.K.: Paternoster/Bible Society, 1995.

France, Richard T. *Translating the Bible: Choosing and Using an English Version.* Cambridge: Grove Books, 1997.

Kubo, Sakae, and Walter Specht. *So Many Versions? Twentieth-Century English Versions of the Bible.* Rev. ed. Grand Rapids: Zondervan, 1983.

Lewis, Jack P. *The English Bible: From KJV to NIV: A History and Evaluation.* 2nd ed. Grand Rapids: Baker, 1991.

Metzger, Bruce M. *The Bible in Translation: Ancient and English Versions.* Grand Rapids: Baker, 2001.

Nida, Eugene A., et al. "Translations." In *The Oxford Companion to the Bible,* edited by B. M. Metzger and M. D. Coogan. Oxford: Oxford University Press, 1993.

Sheeley, Steven M., and Robert N. Nash Jr. *The Bible in English: An Essential Guide.* Nashville: Abingdon Press, 1997.

————. *Choosing a Bible: A Guide to Modern English Translations and Editions.* Nashville: Abingdon Press, 1999.

Skilton, J. H. "English Versions of the Bible." In *The Illustrated Bible Dictionary,* edited by Derek Wood et al. Leicester, U.K.: Inter-Varsity Press, 1980.

Thomas, Robert L. *How to Choose a Bible Version.* Fearn, Ross-shire, U.K.: Christian Focus Publications, 2000.

Zeolla, Gary F. *Differences Between Bible Versions.* Exp. ed. Bloomington, Ind.: First Books Library, 2001.

Translation Theory

Barnwell, Katherine. *Bible Translation: An Introduction Course in Translation Principles.* Summer Institute of Linguistics, 1986.

Beekman, John, and John Callow. *Translating the Word of God.* Grand Rapids: Zondervan, 1974.

de Waard, Jan, and Eugene A. Nida. *From One Language to Another: Functional Equivalence in Bible Translating.* Nashville: Nelson, 1986.

Hargreaves, Cecil. *A Translator's Freedom: Modern English Bibles and Their Language.* Sheffield, U.K.: Sheffield Academic Press, 1993.

Nida, Eugene A. *Towards a Science of Translating.* Leiden, U.K.: Brill/United Bible Societies, 1964.

Nida, Eugene A., and Charles R. Taber. *The Theory and Practice of Translation.* Leiden, U.K.: Brill/United Bible Societies, 1969.

Nida, Eugene A., and William D. Reyburn. *Meaning Across Cultures.* Maryknoll, N.Y.: Orbis, 1981.

Larson, Mildred L. *Meaning-Based Translation.* 2nd ed. Lanham, Md.: University Press of America, 1998.

Louw, Johannes P., ed. *Meaningful Translation: Its Implications for the Reader.* London: United Bible Societies, 1991.

Porter, Stanley, and Richard Hess. *Translating the Bible: Problems and Prospects.* Sheffield, U.K.: Sheffield Academic Press, 1996.

Scorgie, Glen G., Mark L. Strauss and Steven M. Voth, eds. *The Challenge of Bible Translation: Communicating God's Word to the World.* Grand Rapids: Zondervan, 2003.

Wonderly, William L. *Bible Translations for Popular Use.* London: United Bible Societies, 1968.

Gender and Bible Translation

Carson, D. A. *The Inclusive-Language Debate.* Grand Rapids: Baker, 1998.

Grudem, Wayne A., and Vern S. Poythress. *The Gender-Neutral Bible Controversy: Muting the Masculinity of God's Words.* Nashville: Broadman & Holman, 2000.

Strauss, Mark L. *Distorting Scripture? The Challenge of Bible Translation and Gender Accuracy.* Downers Grove, Ill.: InterVarsity Press, 1998.

Hebrew and Greek Text

Bruce, F. F. *The Books and the Parchments.* 3rd ed. London: Pickering & Inglis, 1963.

Metzger, Bruce M. *The Text of the New Testament.* 2nd ed. Oxford: Oxford University Press, 1968.

Patzia, Arthur G. *The Making of the New Testament.* Downers Grove, Ill.: InterVarsity Press, 1995.

Thiede, Carsten Peter. *The Earliest Gospel Manuscript?* Carlisle, U.K.: Paternoster, 1992.

Wolters, Al. "The Text of the Old Testament." In *The Face of Old Testament Studies,* edited by D. W. Baker and B. T Arnold. Grand Rapids: Baker, 1999.

Wurthwein, Ernst. *The Text of the Old Testament.* London: SCM Press, 1980.

Specific Translations

In addition to the explanatory preface of the translations cited in this book, the following relate to the history and translation philosophy of particular translations.

Allis, Oswald T. *Revision or New Translation? The Revised Standard Version of 1946: A Comparative Study.* Philadelphia: Presbyterian & Reformed, 1948.

———. *Revised Version or Revised Bible? A Critique of the Revised Standard Version of the Old Testament.* Philadelphia: Presbyterian & Reformed, 1953.

Barker, Kenneth, ed. *The Making of a Contemporary Translation: New International Version.* London: Hodder & Stoughton, 1991.

Barker, Kenneth. *Accuracy Defined and Illustrated [in the NIV].* Colorado Springs: International Bible Society, 1995.

———. *The Balance of the NIV.* Grand Rapids: Baker, 1999.

Carson, D. A. *The KJV Debate: A Plea for Realism.* Grand Rapids: Baker, 1978.

Coleman, Roger. *New Light and Truth: The Making of the Revised English Bible.* Oxford and Cambridge: Oxford University Press/Cambridge University Press, 1989.

Hunt, Geoffrey, ed. *About the New English Bible.* Oxford and Cambridge: Oxford University Press/Cambridge University Press, 1970.

Martin, Robert. *Accuracy of Translation* [in the NIV]. Edinburgh: Banner of Truth, 1989.

Metzger, Bruce M., Robert C. Dentan and Walter Harrelson. *The Making of the New Revised Standard Version of the Bible.* Grand Rapids: Eerdmans, 1991.

Newman, Barclay M., Charles S. Houser, Erroll F. Rhodes and David G. Burke. *Creating and Crafting the Contemporary English Version.* New York: American Bible Society, 1996.

Phillips, J. B. *Ring of Truth: A Translator's Testimony.* London: Hodder & Stoughton, 1967.

Ryken, Leland. *The Word of God in English: Criteria for Excellence in Bible Translation* [principally ESV]. Wheaton: Crossway, 2002.

Taylor, William Carey. *The New Bible: Pro and Con* [a critical review of the RSV]. New York: Vantage Press, 1955.

Theusen, Peter J. *In Discordance with the Scriptures: American Protestant Battles over Translating the Bible* [mostly about the RSV]. New York: Oxford University Press, 1999.

The Translation Process of God's Word. Cleveland: God's Word to the Nations Bible Society, 1995.

Weigle, Luther A., ed. *An Introduction to the Revised Standard Version of the New Testament.* Nashville: Nelson, 1946.

———. *An Introduction to the Revised Standard Version of the Old Testament.* Nashville: Nelson, 1952.

General

Ackroyd, P. R., and C. F. Evans, eds. *Cambridge History of the Bible*. Cambridge: Cambridge University Press, 1963-1970.

Alter, Robert, and Frank Kermode, eds. *The Literary Guide to the Bible*. London: Collins, 1987; esp. "English Translations of the Bible," by Gerald Hammond.

Brand, Hilary. *The Sceptic's Guide to Reading the Bible*. Oxford: Bible Reading Fellowship, 2000.

Dewey, David. *The Bible Unwrapped*. Milton Keynes: Scripture Union, 2001.

Fee, Gordon D., and Stuart, Douglas. *How to Read the Bible for All Its Worth*, 3rd ed. Grand Rapids: Zondervan, 2003, esp. chap. 2, "The Basic Tool: A Good Translation" is particularly relevant.

Gilmore, Alec. *A Dictionary of the English Bible and Its Origins*. Sheffield, U.K.: Sheffield Academic Press, 2000.

Hamel, Christopher de. *The Book: A History of the Bible*. London: Phaidon, 2001.

Miller, Stephen M., and Robert V. Huber. *The Bible: A History. The Making and Impact of the Bible*. Oxford: Lion, 2003.

Riddell, Mike. *God's Home Page*. Oxford: Bible Reading Fellowship, 1998.

Rogerson, John, ed. *The Oxford Illustrated History of the Bible*. Oxford: Oxford University Press, 2001.